"What I love about Jodie Niznik's (⸻⸻ ⸻⸻ ⸻⸻ ⸻⸻ to Scripture while guiding the studier into the narrative. Placing myself in the situations Moses found himself in helps me better grasp what it means to be a faithful follower today. Niznik's highly practical invitations toward spiritual disciplines further root me in the powerful message that I am loved, God has a plan for my life, and obedience brings joy. This will be a perfect Bible study addition to any ministry longing to deepen women's connection to God."

MARY DEMUTH, author of over forty books,
including *Into the Light*

"What a rich study on the life of Moses! Jodie Niznik offers solid teaching and hands-on application that have the potential to transform us. Filled with outstanding questions and exercises, this study encourages a deep level of engagement. Readers will be prompted to learn from Moses's example, for good or, in some cases, as a cautionary tale in their own walk with God."

NANCY BEACH, leadership coach with the Slingshot Group
and author of *Gifted to Lead*

"Jodie Niznik's writing transcends mere information and targets actual transformation by transparently sharing her own struggles while wisely pointing out how Moses faced real-life issues such as dealing with discouragement, preventing pride's pitfalls, and moving past betrayal. With sensitivity and an ongoing desire to encourage her readers, Jodie introduces each lesson with a spiritual practice to help them in their relationship with the Lord. (My favorites are the first and last practices, rest and celebration!) Let Jodie take you to the next level in your walk with Christ by seriously engaging in this excellent study of Moses's life and ministry."

DR. E. ANDREW MCQUITTY, pastor at large at Irving Bible
Church and author of *The Way to Brave*

"Moses gets the best education in the world and then promptly spends forty years tending sheep on the back side of some desert. That wilderness vocation looks like a colossal waste of purpose—until God shows up in a burning bush. Moses's story is as relevant as ever. And Jodie Niznik is a terrific guide for helping readers see how his story relates to their lives. Through this ten-week inductive Bible study, coupled with spiritual disciplines, Niznik walks readers through what the great prophet's experience can teach us about our own purpose."

DR. SANDRA GLAHN, professor at Dallas Theological
Seminary and author of more than twenty books

"*Choose* offers a highly accessible, deep dive into one of the greatest stories of all time—humanity's move from slavery to freedom. But this is more than just a story. It's an invitation to us all to break free from what binds us and walk in the fullness of Christ."

MARGARET FEINBERG, author of *Fight Back with Joy*
and *More Power to You*

CHOOSE

REAL PEOPLE, REAL FAITH BIBLE STUDIES

Choose: A Study of Moses for a Life That Matters

*Crossroads: A Study of Esther and Jonah for
Boldly Responding to Your Call*

A
REAL PEOPLE,
REAL FAITH
BIBLE STUDY

CHOOSE

A Study of Moses for a Life That Matters

JODIE NIZNIK

KREGEL
PUBLICATIONS

Library of Congress Cataloging-in-Publication Data
Names: Niznik, Jodie, 1973- author.
Title: Choose : a study of Moses for a life that matters / Jodie Niznik.
Description: Grand Rapids, MI : Kregel Publications, 2020. | Series: Real people, real faith Bible studies | Includes bibliographical references.
Identifiers: LCCN 2020015147 (print) | LCCN 2020015148 (ebook)
Subjects: LCSH: Moses (Biblical leader)—Biblical teaching—Textbooks.
Classification: LCC BS580.M6 N59 2020 (print) | LCC BS580.M6 (ebook) | DDC 222/.1092—dc23
LC record available at https://lccn.loc.gov/2020015147
LC ebook record available at https://lccn.loc.gov/2020015148

ISBN 978-0-8254-2568-4, print
ISBN 978-0-8254-7716-4, epub

Printed in the United States of America
20 21 22 23 24 25 26 27 28 29 / 5 4 3 2 1

To my daughters:
may you continue to be bold and brave
as you choose to follow God's lead

CONTENTS

• • • • • •

WHY MOSES AND
WHY NOW?

● ● ● ● ● ● ●

A few years ago, I went through an exhausting season. Every morning I would drag myself out of bed with the goal to just make it through until bedtime. I found myself overloaded and stressed as I was pushed beyond my limits. I was finishing seminary, I had started a new full-time job as a pastor, we were in the process of moving, which meant a new school for my middle school daughters . . . and then the icing on the cake—my husband fell off a ladder and shattered his ankle. Everything seemed to crash in at once. My soul felt dry, my sleep patterns were erratic, and my relationships were taxed. To say I was stressed is an understatement.

Then one day a friend placed a book in my lap. "You need to read this," she said.

I sighed. I didn't have time to sleep, let alone read. I thanked her and placed it on my nightstand, where it sat and stared at me. Finally, on a restless night, I picked it up and started reading. The author introduced me to Moses in a way I hadn't quite seen him before. And it was through this book and some intentional spiritual practices that I started to find rest for my soul again.

Ever since then, I've felt a special kinship to Moses and knew that at some point I wanted to return to his story to really learn from him—his mistakes and successes. I was finally able to do that through preparing this study. Moses's walk with the Lord has become an example to me, beckoning me to follow God in a new way.

As you begin this study of Moses, I pray the same happens for you. I pray the Lord might use Moses's life to become a turning point for you and whatever weariness you are carrying in your soul. And finally, I pray that like Moses you will choose to follow wherever God leads, no matter the costs.

Moses was given one life to live, and while he made some mistakes along the way, he ultimately chose to live it well in surrender to God. You, too, have just one life to live. How will you choose to live it?

—Jodie

WHAT TO EXPECT IN
THIS STUDY

• • • ● • • •

Practice Sections

Each week our lesson will start with a short practice section. The word *practice* is simple and to me expresses the idea that we are just trying something out in our relationship with the Lord. We are practicing. This section will also be a place for us to reflect on the truths we are learning and bring them into our lives in a new way. These practices won't take huge amounts of time, but they may require some planning. Therefore, we will start each week's lesson with the practice section, read it through, and then make a plan to try the suggested activities.

You may discover something you really love in these little sections—something that brings new life into your relationship with the Lord. You may also discover that some of these exercises will take effort. Some may be hard for you to do and others may be easy, even fun! But all of them will help you stretch and grow. Growth almost always brings the spiritual fruit of a changed life. For me, that makes any effort totally worth it. I hope you agree. I'm actually guessing you do. Otherwise, you wouldn't be starting this study.

Pacing Your Study

Each week of this study includes a practice for the week, an introduction to prepare you for the material, and three study sessions. You are welcome to tackle as much of the week's material as you would like on any given day. However, I suggest giving yourself five days to complete the week's work, and I have marked the sections accordingly. If you break it into these chunks, the study shouldn't take you more than thirty minutes to do each day. However, if you are a researcher or extensive reflective thinker, you may want to set aside more time for each day's study.

In general, you will find the days broken down as follows:

Day one will be reading about and planning for the practice activity.

Day two will be preparing for the weekly lesson by reading the introduction and weekly Scripture.

Days three through five will be Scripture reading and answering the questions in this study guide.

If you start running behind (we all have those weeks), you may have to pick and choose which questions you want to answer. My advice is to make the Scripture reading your first priority. Then if you have time, scan through the questions to see which ones you want to answer.

As is usually the case, the higher the investment, the greater the return. When we collaborate with Jesus by inviting him into our lives and spending time with him, we experience life transformation. As your life is transformed, you will find it looking more and more like the life God designed you to live. So make every effort to arrange your days so that you can regularly spend time with Jesus.

GOD IS IN CONTROL

Day 1
Practice—Resting in God

Each week before we start our lesson, I will introduce you to a practice intended to help you take another step in your relationship with the Lord. These brief exercises help you take the head knowledge you are learning from God's Word and move it into heart knowledge.

I know it can be really tempting to skip these if you feel pressed for time, but can I encourage you not to? Sometimes these short activities are exactly what your soul needs. Often they take very little time and just a bit of intentionality.

I think the best way to convince you that these practices are worth your time is to start with my very favorite one—rest. Yes, rest. I'm basically inviting you to take a nap. Aren't you glad you picked up this study?

Think about this: God created us to need rest (Exodus 33:14; Matthew 11:29). He designed humanity to function best when we get adequate sleep. This is not a design flaw; it's a way to help us learn to release control and rely on God to care for us.

Sleep is proven to be essential to good health. The National Sleep Foundation says that while there is no magic number, the average adult needs between seven and nine hours of sleep every night.[1] Unfortunately, they have also found that 49 percent of American adults have sleep-related problems, and one in six suffers from chronic insomnia. And even if we can fall asleep and make it through the night, many of us still press the boundaries of adequate sleep by staying up too late or getting up too early.

So how are you doing with sleep? Are you getting enough? And if not, why not?

This week, I want to challenge you to take some action, or more accurately some nonaction, and get some rest. To do this, plan one day to sleep until you wake up. Allow your body to rest until it is done. I realize this will probably take some planning. If you have small children at home, you may need to make arrangements with a spouse or a friend to help you. If you wake in the middle of the night, try not to get frustrated that you've ruined your sleep activity. Instead, I recommend you slowly and meditatively recite a verse that helps you surrender to and trust in the Lord. Lately I've been reciting, "The LORD is my shepherd, I have all that I need" (Psalm 23:1 NLT). It reminds me that God sees me and will provide for all my needs . . . even sleep.

Of course, there are always legitimate seasons when we can't get enough rest—such as being a new mom or experiencing a family crisis. If you find yourself in one of these seasons, prayerfully consider who you might be able to ask to give you a few days of relief so you can recharge with some good rest. And if that isn't possible, try to do a few nights where you intentionally choose to go to bed as early as possible and sleep as late as you can. The key is, put a plan in place and try it. If that plan doesn't work, try another one.

As you rest, I hope you also discover a much deeper spiritual practice—trust. Trust isn't just something *we* need to learn, as we will see it is exactly what the Israelites needed to learn too. They found themselves bound in backbreaking slavery and needed to trust that God had not forgotten them even though the situation felt bleak. No matter what's happening in your life right now, resting can be a physical cue to help you remember that God has not lost sight of you either. It is through rest that we learn to trust in and surrender to God and the limits he has designed us with. Rest also helps us remember that the world doesn't depend on us, it depends on God. We can rest because God never rests. And if you discover you really can't find the time for adequate rest, ask him to help you discern what needs to change.

Just as he had for Moses, God has an amazing plan for your life, a plan that fits within your God-given limitations. Use all the tools he's provided for you, like rest, and you will be ready for the task.

Take a few minutes to prayerfully make a plan for how you will rest this week. Write it down, noting any action steps you need to take and when you will take them. (For example, "I will talk to my family today about sleeping until I wake up Saturday morning and what we all need to do to help that happen.")

"God created us in His image. He is a God who works and then rests. When we rest we honor the way God made us. Rest can be a spiritual act—a truly human act of submission to and dependence on God who watches over all things as we rest."
—Adele Ahlberg Calhoun[2]

Day 2
Preparation

Read Exodus 1:1–2:25.

> *As you read this passage, write down anything that stands out to you along with any questions you may have.*

Just because you've picked up a study on Moses, I don't want to assume you know who he is. So let's take a moment to get to know a few things about him. Many scholars agree that Moses was born sometime near 1400 BC. The Bible confirms that he lived for 120 years, during the period that the Hebrews, who were God's people, were enslaved by the Egyptians. The Egyptians, as you will discover, were unrelenting taskmasters. They had built an entire economy and lavish lifestyle on the backs of the nearly two million Hebrew slaves. All of this was overseen by the evil Egyptian king (called the pharaoh).

The Hebrews, who had finally reached their breaking point, cried out to God for deliverance. God heard their cries and sent Moses to rescue them. Rescuing the people wasn't an easy task, though. The pharaoh didn't want his entire workforce to walk away, so he resisted Moses's repeated requests to free the Hebrew people. This started a deadly and destructive back-and-forth battle. In the end, the pharaoh failed and God's people found freedom.

One of the things this story shows us is that nothing can thwart God's ultimate plan. If he says he will do something, then he will do it. He is stronger and more powerful than any pharaoh will ever be.

While we do not find ourselves ruled by a tyrant pharaoh as in Moses's day, there are still many things that try to enslave us by holding us back from God's best. People, circumstances, and even our own thoughts can begin to act like personal mini-pharaohs when they distract us from God's good plans for our lives. And often the biggest pharaoh we struggle with is ourselves.

I frequently struggle with my thoughts. In mere seconds I can go from boldly believing God is calling me to do something to rationalizing my way out of it. I start to tell myself lies like: I probably heard him wrong; I don't have time; I'm not good enough; I'll surely fail; or I just don't know where to start. And I often think all of these things at the same time. I know I'm not alone; you do this too. The lies we often allow ourselves to think can rule over us and hold us in bondage, keeping us away from God's best. We may not be struggling with physical slavery as the Hebrews were, but we still need to battle against the pharaohs that threaten us today.

The good news is, God is always ready to tell us the truth about these pharaohs. The truth is, our pharaohs are no match for God. God is good and sovereign, and you can rest in his control. God is waiting and ready for us to say yes to his plans. And just like Moses, he has a good plan for your life.

What pharaoh is standing in your way?

May this lesson give you courage that God is in control, and just like he handled the pharaoh of Moses's day, he can handle the pharaohs that try to stand in your way today.

PRACTICE REMINDER

If you haven't done so already, practice rest this week by planning one day to sleep until you wake up.

Day 3
Israelites Enslaved in Egypt

Read Exodus 1:1–21.

The story of Moses begins in the book of Exodus, the second book of the Bible. But before we can understand what's happening in Exodus, we need to grab some history from Genesis, the first book of the Bible. Genesis is a book that tells the story of creation, humans falling into sin, and God electing Israel as his chosen people. It is also worth noting up front that God's chosen people were referred to by a few names other than just Israel. They were also called Hebrews and Jews. Each term had significance and came about at a different time in history but refers to the same group of people—God's chosen people.

The story of God's people is a tumultuous one. A few hundred years before Moses, God covenanted with Abraham and his descendants to never leave or forsake them, yet they continually turned away from God. And while God held to his covenant with them, there were still consequences for their disobedience. God warned them that trouble would eventually come. He said, "Know for certain that for four hundred years your descendants will be strangers in a country not their own and that they will be enslaved and mistreated there" (Genesis 15:13).

Is *pharaoh* a name or a title? Pharaoh is a title. The Bible commonly uses it to denote a king of Egypt. A synonym for pharaoh could be "his honor" or "his majesty."[3]

A few generations later, as the book of Genesis closed, these words came to pass. The Israelites moved to the foreign land of Egypt where they were "strangers in a country not their own." Exodus 1:1–7 described these first four hundred years of Israel living in Egypt as a fruitful time where they experienced an Israelite population explosion. After that time, however, they became "enslaved and mistreated there." The entire nation of Israel was now enslaved to Egypt. This is where Moses entered the story.

1. Read Exodus 1:6–11.

What happened to Joseph and his brothers? (As a little background, Joseph is a significant Israelite who facilitated the nation moving to Egypt in a time of dire famine. This move saved the entire nation from destruction. You can read his full story in Genesis 37–50.) Based on Genesis 41:41–43, why do you think this is significant?

What happened to the Israelites?

Is there anything else that stands out to you in this passage?

2. Hebrew slave labor had become an important part of the Egyptian economy. What could have been the implications to the Egyptians and the pharaoh himself if the Israelites had left?

3. According to verses 9–10, one of the king's biggest concerns was the growing number of Israelites. What do you think the pharaoh was hoping would happen once he enslaved the people? What happened instead (1:12)? How did the Egyptians respond (1:12–14)?

4. The king decided to try a different tactic. According to verses 15–16, what did he ask the midwives to do? What did the midwives do instead, and why did they do this (1:17)?

The fear of God can be a hard concept for us to grasp. We often use the word "fear" in a negative way to describe something that grips us with terror or dread. Yet there is also a positive definition of *fear*. If you read deep enough into the dictionary definitions, you'll find it is also defined as having a reverential awe of God.[4]

5. Read Psalm 34:8–14 and Proverbs 8:13. Practically speaking, what does it look like to fear God today? What are some ways you can do this?

6. Scripture tells us the midwives feared God, but do you think they also feared the pharaoh? If so, why? How might their fear of the pharaoh have differed from their fear of God? Why do you think they ultimately feared God more than the pharaoh?

Proverbs 9:10 says, "The fear of the LORD is the beginning of wisdom, and knowledge of the Holy One is understanding."

The midwives were placed in an impossible situation as they were asked to do the unthinkable. They knew that if the pharaoh was willing to kill innocent newborns, then he wouldn't think twice about killing them. They had to make a choice, and no matter what choice was made, lives were on the line. Their choice to fear God over Pharaoh took a lot of courage. This is a clear and extreme example of being asked to do something by a human authority that goes against the will of God.

I'm inspired by the courage of the midwives. They risked their lives by choosing to obey God and disobey the pharaoh. The stakes were high either way. They remind me that obedience to God is always worth it. This life is temporary. Keeping an eternal perspective helps me find courage to follow God no matter the possible costs. —Jodie

7. Have you (or someone you know) ever been asked to do something by an authority figure that you believe was wrong and therefore went against God's will? Describe the situation. What did you (or the other person) do?

If you were faced with the situation again, what, if anything, would you do differently?

8. What ultimately happened to the midwives (1:20–21)?

How does this encourage you to rest in God's control even when circumstances seem to tell you otherwise?

Ultimately things worked out well for the midwives. Their lives were spared and they were blessed with their own families. However, we aren't promised a happy ending when we make the hard choice to fear and obey God instead of people. Scripture and recent history tell us that there are many who have endured incredibly difficult circumstances and even lost their lives as a result of choosing to follow God. Jesus, who followed God perfectly, is a great example of this truth. His path led to a torturous death at the hands of his enemies. We aren't promised that when we make the right choice things will always work out as we might wish.

9. Read Jesus's words in John 16:33. What did he say about troubles? Where can we find peace and why? How does this encourage you in troubles you are currently facing?

☀

"The important principle emerges here that God will honour those who defend the principles of righteousness, showing respect for his creation and his rule over life. The midwives are more anxious to please God than to please Pharaoh, and God rewards them."

—Iain D. Campbell[5]

PRACTICE REMINDER

If you haven't done so already, practice rest this week by planning one day to sleep until you wake up.

Day 4
Moses Is Born

Read Exodus 1:22–2:10; Acts 7:18–22.

Up to this point, the pharaoh tried to control the Israelite population through backbreaking labor and oppression and the attempted killing of all newborn baby boys. These two tactics did not work and so he tried a third way. He ordered every Hebrew boy be thrown into the Nile River. It is in the midst of this order that Moses's mother conceives and gives birth.

10. Read Exodus 2:1–9.

    What did Moses's mother notice about him?

    Why do you think she could no longer hide him after he was three months old?

The pharaoh's daughter finds Moses at the river and asks Moses's sister, who was watching everything unfold, to find someone to care for and nurse him. Why do you think the pharaoh's daughter does this? What else do we learn about Moses's upbringing from Acts 7:22? Why do you think this could be significant?

Is there anything else that stands out to you about Exodus 2:1–9?

Throughout our study, I will offer the opportunity for us to use our imaginations in a sanctified way. These "imagine" questions are intended to help us enter into the story and remember that the people we are studying were real people with real emotions, hopes, and fears. In my own spiritual journey, the Lord has used these kinds of activities to draw my attention to ideas, feelings, or circumstances that have both encouraged and challenged me. However, I also want to offer a word of caution. We never want to impose our own ideas on the text. We can't know what someone is thinking or feeling unless the text tells us. We also need to remember these biblical characters lived in a very different culture and age than we do. So as you imagine what it might have been like for someone, just remember we can never truly know. We might be able to make some good assumptions, but until we meet them in heaven and ask them what they were really thinking and feeling, we need to hold it loosely.

11. Take a moment to try to imagine what it would be like if you were Moses's mother. Write what you might have thought and felt as you made each of the choices illustrated below.

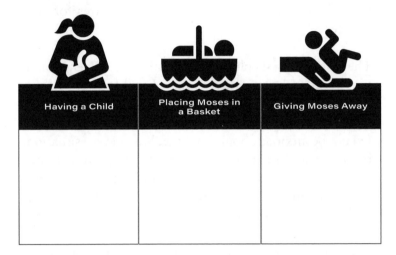

Having a Child	Placing Moses in a Basket	Giving Moses Away

12. What do you learn about how Moses's mother handled the situation from Hebrews 11:23?

Moses's mother had no idea how things would turn out when she placed him in the river. She acted in faith and did what she thought was best. Moses's life was ultimately spared through her actions, but it was still a bittersweet outcome as she had to give Moses over to be raised by someone else.

13. What situation(s) in your life has you worried because you are unsure of the ultimate outcome? Describe the situation and why it concerns you.

14. Read the following verses. Underline what we should do with our anxiety and concerns. Circle the reason why or the way we should do this.

Cast all your anxiety on him because he cares for you. (1 Peter 5:7)

The LORD is my shepherd, I lack nothing. . . . Even though I walk through the darkest valley, I will fear no evil, for you are with me. (Psalm 23:1, 4)

Do not be anxious about anything, but in every situation, by prayer and petition, with thanksgiving, present your requests to God. And the peace of God, which transcends all understanding, will guard your hearts and your minds in Christ Jesus. (Philippians 4:6–7)

Based on the Philippians verses, what will result when we give these concerns over to God and rest in his control over life?

Based on the model of praying in Philippians 4:6–7, write a short prayer about the situation you identified in question 13. Start by thanking God for what is good and then present your request to him. Ask him to provide the peace he promises he will.

I don't know where you find yourself today, I am wrestling with peace. And this reminds me of the uncertainty in my world that evolved with COVID-19. When everyone was ordered to stay at home, my husband was an essential employee, so he was at work. My daughters lived in different states with roommates who were handling this virus with varying degrees of seriousness. My illusion of control was shattered, as it was for most.

As I read these verses with fresh eyes today, I am reminded that the peace God is offering isn't a reassurance that all will be well as the world qualifies it. No, the peace God is providing me today is the reminder that he is my good shepherd and I truly do have all I need in him. And all I need is much less than I thought it was.

Maybe you are wrestling with peace today too. If so, know that I'm praying that "the peace of God, which transcends all understanding" will settle deep into your heart right now.

15. God chose to protect Moses through the choices and actions of different people. Who were these people and what do they have in common (1:17; 2:2, 5–7)?

How does this encourage you? When circumstances have felt overwhelming, how have you seen God's protection and care in the choices and actions of the people God has put in your life?

Day 5
Moses at Forty

Read Exodus 2:11–25; Acts 7:23–29.

Moses was raised as the son of the pharaoh's daughter—which
made him like a grandson to the pharaoh. The text doesn't tell us
who really knew about Moses's true identity, but it does indicate
that Moses knew he was really a Hebrew. When he was forty
years old, and presumably still living in the pharaoh's household,
he witnessed an Israelite being beaten by an Egyptian. Seeing
that no one was around, he killed the Egyptian and buried him
in the sand. The next day he witnessed two Israelites fighting
against each other and he decided to intervene again.

16. According to Acts 7:25, what was Moses's motive in inter-
    vening? Based on how the Israelites react to Moses (Exodus
    2:14; Acts 7:27–28), what do you think they thought of
    Moses? If they knew he was a Hebrew, why do you think
    they didn't want his help?

17. Do you think Moses's method of intervening was misguided? Why or why not?

Think back to a time in your life when you had a good motive but had a poor method. What happened? Why do you think your method was wrong? How might have remembering that ultimate deliverance lies with God have allowed you to approach the issue more effectively?

18. How does Pharaoh respond when he hears about what Moses has done (Exodus 2:15)?

How many times has Pharaoh tried to kill Moses up to this point (Exodus 1:16, 22; 2:15)? The text doesn't tell us if Pharaoh knew if Moses was a Hebrew or not, but at least in this last attempted killing, we can assume the pharaoh does know he was raised as his daughter's son. Considering this, why do you think he responded so harshly?

19. According to Job 14:5, Psalm 139:16, and Proverbs 19:21, why didn't the pharaoh succeed in killing Moses? How does this truth encourage or comfort you?

※

"Many are the plans in a person's heart, but it is the LORD's purpose that prevails." (Proverbs 19:21)

20. While we are not always promised to be protected, we often are. In your life, where have you seen God's protection and preservation? Tell about a specific time.

21. When bad things happen in our lives, what does Romans 8:28 say God will do? (Notice: Romans doesn't say the thing that has happened is good.) Where have you experienced this truth in your life? How does this promise free you to rest more fully in God's sovereign control of your life?

It's important to remember that bad things can happen in our lives for many reasons. Sometimes it's the consequences of our own actions (like getting in an accident because we ran a red light), sometimes it's just because we got caught in the consequences of someone else's wrong actions (like getting hit by someone who ran a red light), and sometimes it's really no fault of our own but just because we live in a broken world marred by the effects

"For 40 years (Acts 7:30) Moses undertook the toilsome life of a sheepherder in the Sinai area, thus gaining valuable knowledge of the topography of the Sinai Peninsula which later was helpful as he led the Israelites in that wilderness land."

—John D. Hannah[6]

of sin (like getting sick). The important thing to remember is that God never causes these bad things to happen. He does allow them at times, but he never causes them. And when these hard things do intersect our lives, remember that our good Father promises to be with us every step of the way. He will never leave us or forsake us (Deuteronomy 31:6).

We leave Moses in Midian, a dry and desolate desert land. There he met and married Zipporah and they had two sons. He spent the next forty years in the desert of Midian as a shepherd. Forty years seems like a long time to us, and it is. We don't know much of what happened during those years, but we can be sure the time was not wasted. God was most certainly preparing Moses for his calling to rescue his people. And God was also preparing his people to be ready to follow Moses.

No matter where you find yourself today, you can rest in the truth that, like Moses, you have been chosen by God. He is able to use everything in your life to prepare you for your chosen journey. Stay focused on him and continue to follow where he leads.

PRACTICE REFLECTION

1. What was this rest activity like for you? What did you enjoy about it? What was hard about it?

2. What did you notice about the day after you rested adequately (your reactions, productivity, alertness, etc.)?

3. Is this something you desire to keep doing? What adjustments would need to be made in your life to accomplish this?

BURNING BUSH MOMENTS

Day 1
Practice—Paying Attention

As we learned in the last lesson, Moses was a shepherd in the desert of Midian for forty years. I'm guessing after forty years of doing the same work on the same land, he had pretty much seen it all. That was until the day he came across a bush in flames. Perhaps a burning bush wasn't all that abnormal in a dry, hot place, but the longer he looked the more he noticed that the bush didn't seem to burn up. When he went over to see what was going on, that's when something extraordinary happened—God spoke to him through the bush. I can't even imagine. If I saw a bush in flames, I would be startled. But if the bush spoke to me, I would start running the other direction and probably call 911—for myself and the bush.

Truthfully, I'm not sure how I would react to such an overt and obvious calling by God. I might think my mind was playing tricks on me. And yet I long for this kind of clear and direct leading from the Lord. I know many of us do. While God could certainly speak in an audible voice to tell us his will, that doesn't

35

seem to be the way he does things today. But I do think God still sends us burning-bush moments as he regularly sets ordinary things ablaze with his activity. Unfortunately, we are often prone to pass by these moments without pausing to notice.

This week, we are going to intentionally pause to pay attention by doing a spiritual practice believers have been doing for centuries called "the daily examen." The examen is a useful tool that can help us discern God's will as we pause, reflect, and notice patterns in our lives.

To do this daily examen, take five to ten minutes first thing in the morning or right before bedtime to prayerfully reflect back over the last twenty-four hours. I've provided five questions below to help you do this. You'll notice that I ask you to pay attention to things that are both life-giving and life-draining. This isn't for the purpose of scratching all those life-draining things off your list, although there may be some things you should stop doing. The purpose is to pay attention to why they bring energy or seem to pull it away. Neither is inherently good or bad. They are simply things we need to pay attention to.

For example, my bills don't pay themselves, my email inbox doesn't miraculously jump to zero, and clean clothes don't magically appear in my closet. I know these things still need to be done, and so I ask the Lord to help me consider why they feel life-draining, and then I ask him to help me find a new way and new attitude for doing these things. Perhaps it isn't that email is actually life-draining; rather, it's the fact that I've let it invade my life without good boundaries. I tend to check my phone and send off a quick reply at all hours. It feels harmless, even productive, but it's actually draining. Recognizing this has helped me set boundaries that have led to life-giving rhythms of work and rest. I still have to do email, but I try to choose to do it in a way that feels much more life-giving.

I also ask you to pay attention to your body and what it seems to be telling you. I often like to say that my body tells the truth on me. I may think I feel fine, but when my shoulders are knotted up and I'm not sleeping through the night, I need to take a deeper look at what's going on.

The most important question on the examen is the last one. It asks if we sensed God leading us to do something and how we responded to this leading. Keeping a short account with ourselves by daily paying attention to what we think God is inviting us to can become a life-transforming practice. This is why I ask you to write these things down each day so you can start to see patterns. We are forgetful people. We can move past God's leading and forget it even happened by the next day. I know I can. Writing these things down helps me see what I'm resisting or responding to and why. I often begin to see patterns emerge and this helps me discern more clearly what God may be leading me to.

The examen isn't a magic formula for knowing God's will though. It is simply a way to help you slow down and notice. A way to help you see if there are any burning bushes in your life. If you do notice something, can I encourage you to follow Moses's lead by stopping to listen and pay attention? Ask the Holy Spirit what he wants you to see and how he wants you to respond. And then take the leap of faith and follow where you sense he is leading.

The Daily Examen

1. What energized me in the last twenty-four hours?

Day 1

Picking up Lucy!

Day 2

Day 3

Day 4

Day 5

2. Where did I feel the least energy? What were the circumstances of this situation?

Day 1

Day 2

Day 3

Day 4

Day 5

3. What has my physical body been telling me?

Day 1

Day 2

Day 3

Day 4

Day 5

4. What was I most grateful for over the last twenty-four
hours?

Day 1

Day 2

Day 3

Day 4

Day 5

5. Did I sense God leading me in the last twenty-four hours?
   Did I cooperate or resist? Why?

   Day 1

   Day 2

Day 3

Day 4

Day 5

Day 2
Preparation

Read Exodus 2:23–3:22.

> *As you read this passage, write down anything that stands out to you along with any questions you may have.*

I believe we all want our lives to deeply matter. If you asked me, I would initially tell you that I would love it if God called me to do something miraculous and world-changing—and if he could speak to me with an audible voice from a burning bush, it would be even better. But I also wonder, if he really did call me to do something like this, how would I really react?

When Moses got his significant, not-to-be-missed calling from

God, I think it's helpful to observe how he reacted. He didn't say, "Finally. I've been waiting for you to tell me what to do. Let's get going." No, Moses hid, he asked some questions, he worked out some things within his soul, and he wrestled with whether he even wanted to be obedient. A reality check tells me that I would probably react like Moses did. I bet you would too.

While God can speak however he wants, we probably won't get a physical burning bush or an audible voice. However, we do get something I would argue is even better. We have the indwelling Holy Spirit who is always with us, guiding us into God's will. Scripture tells us that the Holy Spirit makes God's will clear to us just when we need to know it (John 14:15–17; 16:13–14; 1 Corinthians 2:9–13).

My calling to attend seminary happened this way. I wasn't even thinking of going back to school until one day when I was at a conference and I had a burning-bush moment when I heard the Spirit speak these words into my heart and mind: "I want you to go to seminary." I literally looked at the woman sitting next to me to see if she had heard it too. I was stunned. This was definitely not a thought I would think on my own. I started praying and paying attention. God affirmed this initial calling to me in multiple ways. One way was through his provision. We couldn't afford tuition and then he provided in multiple miraculous ways—a sacrificial gift from a friend, an unexpected scholarship, and a just-enough-to-cover-the-costs promotion for my husband. God also affirmed his calling by changing my heart and giving me the desire and excitement to go back to school. I'm glad he did, because seminary was hard and it was a significant sacrifice for my whole family.

When Moses was called, he had to decide if he was going to follow in obedience. As Moses followed, God proved himself faithful over and over. The journey wasn't easy. In fact, it was long and hard. But it was an adventure and a calling that made Moses's life really matter. We are invited to make similar decisions in our lives. Will we choose to follow God in obedience when he calls? Like Moses, our journey probably won't be easy, but God will prove himself to be faithful in it. And obedience to God is an adventure that is always worth taking.

PRACTICE REMINDER

If you haven't done so already, take a few minutes
to practice the daily examen beginning on page 37.

Day 3
Called to Freedom

Read Exodus 2:23–3:1.

In the last lesson, we learned that Moses fled Egypt and settled
in the desert of Midian. Acts 7:30 tells us that forty years passed,
which means Moses would have been eighty years old in this
next passage. It also means the Israelites remained enslaved in
Egypt over those last forty years.

1. What do these verses tell us about each of the following
   characters?

   The pharaoh

   The Israelites

   God

2. What is Moses doing (most likely as his occupation) in Exodus 3:1? What does Genesis 46:34 tell us about how the Egyptians viewed shepherds? Considering Moses was raised for forty years as an Egyptian, how do you think this might have impacted how he felt about his vocation?

3. Review Acts 7:23–29. These verses seem to indicate that Moses somehow knew God intended to use him to rescue the Israelites. Forty years have passed since Moses attempted to enact a "rescue" on his own terms—which resulted in the sin of murdering an Egyptian. Do you think Moses still believed God could or would want to use him to rescue his people? Why or why not? If not, what do you think he believed about himself while he was in Midian?

John 8:34 says, "Everyone who sins is a slave to sin." Considering this, both Moses and the Israelites were enslaved. Moses was enslaved spiritually due to his sins of acting outside of God's will and murder. The nation of Israel was enslaved physically. God in his graciousness wanted to release both Moses and the nation of Israel from their slavery. He wants to do the same for us too. By faith in Jesus, God releases us from spiritual bondage to sin and physical bondage to death.

4. Is there any sin from your past that continues to weigh on you? How could you be allowing that sin to hold you back instead of feeling released to move forward in your relationship and calling with God? (This question is for personal reflection. You will not be asked to share this in your small group discussion time.)

5. What do the following verses tell us about our sin once we become a Christian? Circle all the words that describe us as Christians.

Therefore, if anyone is in Christ, the new creation has come: The old is gone, the new is here! (2 Corinthians 5:17)

If we confess our sins, he is faithful and just and will forgive us our sins and purify us from all unrighteousness. (1 John 1:9)

As far as the east is from the west, so far has he removed our transgressions from us. (Psalm 103:12)

If you struggle to believe that these truths apply to you, why do you think that is? (If you are uncertain you are a Christian, please reach out to your group leader or a trusted Christian friend to discuss this with them.)

PRACTICE REMINDER

If you haven't done so already, take a few minutes
to practice the daily examen beginning on page 37.

Day 4
Calling and Questions

Read Exodus 3:2–15.

6. What does Moses see and do? Why does he think it is
strange (3:2–3)?

7. Exodus 3:4 is the first time God speaks to Moses. What
does God say? Why do you think this is significant?

"This was the first time God had revealed himself to Moses, or
anyone else as far as Scripture records, for over 430 years (v. 4).
. . . Later in history God broke another 400-year-long period
of prophetic silence when John the Baptist and Jesus appeared
to lead an even more significant 'exodus.' God raised up Jesus,
another outcast, to lead His people out of bondage."

—Dr. Thomas L. Constable[1]

8. According to Exodus 3:5–6, Moses hid his face because he was afraid to look at God. Why do you think he was afraid?

9. If God appeared to you in a burning bush, how do you think you would react? Would you hide your face from God? Why or why not?

10. According to Exodus 3:7–11, God tells Moses he has seen the Israelites' misery and is going to rescue them. Why do you think Moses responds the way that he does? How do you think you would respond if you were Moses?

11. Has there ever been a time in your life when you felt a strong calling by God to do something? Describe the situation and how you responded.

12. How does God reply to Moses in 3:12? Does God really answer Moses's question? Why do you think God answers this way?

"Moses had asked, 'Who am I?' implying his complete inadequacy for his calling. God replied, 'I am who I am!' implying his complete adequacy. The issue was not who Moses was, but who God is. I believe God meant, 'I am the God of your forefathers who proved myself long ago . . . so it really doesn't matter who you are, Moses.'"

—Dr. Thomas L. Constable[2]

13. In Exodus 3:13–15, what does Moses ask God this second time? List the three ways God identifies himself to Moses. What do you think this says about God?

It's important to note that Jesus also calls himself the "I am" (John 8:58). He uses this intentional word choice to echo Exodus 3:14 and clearly makes the claim that he is God. The Jews listening to him understood what these words meant and picked up stones to kill him because they thought it was blasphemous (Leviticus 24:16).
—Jodie

If you haven't done so already, take a few minutes to practice the daily examen beginning on page 37.

Day 5
Next Steps

Read Exodus 3:16–22.

14. Moses is to go tell the elders of Israel what God has seen and what God plans to do. How does God say the elders will receive Moses and what are they supposed to do next (3:18)? What will God do to compel the pharaoh to let them go (3:19–20)?

15. What do you notice about the level of details God gives Moses when he tells him the next steps to take? Why do you think this is?

Look back at your response to question 11. What level of details did God give you for what he was calling you to do? Do you think it would have been more or less helpful to know more details? Why or why not?

16. Review Acts 7:20–36 and write a brief summary of Moses's life in the boxes below. Put a star where Moses encountered God at the burning bush. How old was he? Does this seem old to you? Why?

Birth–40	40–80	80–120

If you live to be ninety-nine years old and your life is structured similarly to Moses's (in terms of when God called you for a significant task), that would make you sixty-six at the time of your burning bush moment. Mark your current age and the age you decided to follow Christ. Does this encourage you or discourage you? Why?

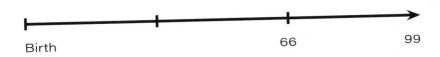

Birth   66   99

17. God used an audible voice in a burning bush to speak to Moses. While God can speak to us audibly, it is not the normative way God chooses to speak to us today. How do we hear from God today? Read through the following verses and underline how God speaks. The first one is done for you.

If you aren't familiar with Moses's entire story, you will discover that God uses him until the last day of his life. So no matter your age, as long as you have breath in your lungs, be assured that God has purposeful plans for you. Keep trusting in him and he will lead you. —Jodie

A voice came from the cloud, saying, "This is my Son, whom I have chosen; listen to him." (Luke 9:35)

Do not merely listen to the word, and so deceive yourselves. Do what it says. (James 1:22)

But when he, the Spirit of truth, comes, he will guide you into all the truth. He will not speak on his own; he will speak only what he hears, and he will tell you what is yet to come. (John 16:13)

In the past God spoke to our ancestors through the prophets at many times and in various ways, but in these last days he has spoken to us by his Son, whom he appointed heir of all things, and through whom also he made the universe. (Hebrews 1:1–2)

All Scripture is God-breathed and is useful for teaching, rebuking, correcting and training in righteousness. (2 Timothy 3:16)

"The Five Ms of Correctly Hearing God: 1. Look for the message of the Spirit. 2. Live in the mode of prayer. 3. Search out the model of Scripture. 4. Submit to the ministry of [a wise, more mature believer who can discern God's leading in his or her own life]. 5. Expect the mercy of confirmation."

—Priscilla Shirer[3]

Using the chart below, summarize the three ways these Scriptures teach us that God speaks to us, then write how we actually "hear" these voices.

Way God Speaks	How We Hear
1. Through Jesus (God's Son)	Through his words recorded in Scripture
2.	
3.	

❋

"In our day, God speaks to us through the Holy Spirit. He uses the Bible, prayer, circumstances and the church (other believers). No one of these methods of God's speaking is, by itself, a clear indicator of God's directions. But when God says the same things through each of these ways, you can have confidence to proceed."

—Henry Blackaby[4]

Let me leave you with this quote from Priscilla Shirer's *Discerning the Voice of God* as we finish our lesson:

> The Holy Spirit will never tell us to do anything that isn't in God's will. He speaks exactly what he hears from the Father. He begins to influence our minds, will, emotions, and bodies to desire what is pleasing to God and will bring him glory. Our responsibility is to cooperate by obeying his promptings and bathing ourselves in the Word and in prayer.[5]

Perhaps your moments of calling have not been as dramatic as Moses's encounter with the burning bush. But if you feel the Holy Spirit prompting you in some way, can I encourage you to pay attention? And then take a step forward in obedience. God will not let you down—He will continue to lead you. The journey won't always be easy, but it is always worth it.

PRACTICE REFLECTION

1. Review your notes from the Paying Attention practice we did this week. Do you notice any patterns?

2. Do you sense the Holy Spirit calling you toward or away from something? If so, what? Why do you think this is?

THE COMFORT OF CONFIRMATION

Day 1
Practice—Gratitude Journal

When hard circumstances come into my life, I usually start by asking God things like: What do you want me to do? How should I respond? What is the best next step? I also find that in the beginning of a hard season I ask him to shape my words, my heart, and my thoughts. The problem is that while I often start from a place that is surrendered to him and his will, I often lack the stamina to stay in this surrendered posture. If the circumstance drags on—or if hard things continue to pile up—I revert to questions that have a different tone.

What if I can't figure this out? What if I make the wrong choice? What if these circumstances don't change?

These what-if questions expose my heart of fear and self-reliance versus God-reliance. The problem isn't the questions in themselves; God can handle any question we ask. The problem is they are exposing that I'm drifting away from trusting in God.

When I notice this starting to happen, one of the best remedies

I've found is to intentionally ask God to help me remember what is really true. Paul tells us that thinking about the true things of God is actually the antidote to fear and worry. He says, "Whatever is true, whatever is noble, whatever is right, whatever is pure, whatever is lovely, whatever is admirable—if anything is excellent or praiseworthy—think about such things. . . . And the God of peace will be with you" (Philippians 4:8–9). Did you catch that? The God of peace will be with you. We are actually promised peace when we think about the true things of God. Peace is the exact opposite of fear and worry.

One practical way I've discovered to think about the true things of God is through the practice of keeping a gratitude journal. Each morning before I start my time with Jesus, I take a few moments to reflect back over the previous day and write down three things I was grateful for. I try to be specific and to make it unique. So instead of saying I'm grateful for my home, I might say I'm grateful for the comfortable pillow I get to sleep on each night. Or that I'm grateful for the laundry I just put in the wash because it means I have more than enough clothing and laundry detergent to wash them with.

This week, I want to invite you to take a few moments each day to write in your own gratitude journal and see how it impacts your heart posture. To do this, we will seek to notice fifty unique things that are worthy of praise. I recommend you do this every day by writing down seven to ten specific things you are grateful for. I want to encourage you to do this daily instead of all at once because there's something unique and soul-filling that happens in our hearts and minds when we engage with this practice regularly. In fact, there's a whole field of study called positive psychology that has proven that this type of daily practice actually changes our outlook on life from negative to positive—from worry to peace. Don't you love it when science points out something we already know is true from Scripture?

As you notice all God has done for you, I pray your heart will be renewed with undivided trust in him. And as this trust takes deeper root, may your fears and doubts fade to the background, leaving you willing and ready to follow wherever he is leading.

Gratitude Journal

1._____

2._____

3._____

4._____

5._____

6._____

7._____

8._____

9._____

10._____

11._____

12._____

13._____

14._____

15._____

16._____

17._____

18._____

19._____

20._____

21._____

22._____

23._____

24._____

25._____

26._____

27._____

28._____

29._____

30._____

31._____

32._____

33._____

34._____

35._____

36._____

37._____

38._____

39._____

40._____

41._____

42._____

43._____

44._____

45._____

46._____

47._____

48._____

49._____

50._____

Day 2
Preparation

Read Exodus 4:1–31.

> *As you read this passage, write down anything that stands out to you along with any questions you may have.*

In last week's lesson we looked at Moses's calling from God and how God speaks to us today. But how do we respond to God's calling, and how can we be assured of our ability to follow his leading? Moses responded as many of us would—with a few questions. His first question focused on a legitimate concern: "Who am I that I should go to Pharaoh and bring the Israelites out of Egypt?" (Exodus 3:11). While we can't know for certain, it seems this question addressed Moses's concern for his reputation and ability to complete such a monumental task. Don't forget, Moses had made a mess of his life when he murdered a man and fled to the desert to hide. With this in mind, it certainly seems that the real question Moses asked was if God could really use him in spite of all he had done.

I get it. I've had similar conversations with God where I've wondered if I was really the right person for the task. What God has reminded me in these situations is that it isn't about me; it's about God. And the same was true for Moses. God reminded Moses of this truth when he said, "I will be with you" (Exodus 3:12). With this statement, Moses was invited to trust in the one who was sending him.

This response led to a second seemingly honest question from Moses: Who should I tell them you are? God responded: "Say to the Israelites: 'I AM has sent me to you'" (Exodus 3:14). In this short phrase, God named himself the "I AM." While books have been written that explore this God-size "I AM" statement and name, it simply, and yet complexly, means he is all and everything and he can be depended on. And when the all and everything I AM sends, we need to go. He sent Moses and he also sends us.

Many Scriptures affirm the truth that we are also sent. And while we obviously won't be sent on the same assignment as Moses, God has specific things he invites us to do—things that only we can do. Ephesians 2:10 and Jeremiah 29:11 are two of my favorite verses that support this truth. Take a moment to read them (in the margin) and let

For we are God's masterpiece. He has created us anew in Christ Jesus, so we can do the good things he planned for us long ago. (Ephesians 2:10 NLT)

their truths wash over you. God has planned work for you to do—work he created long ago. The I AM invites you to be a part of his holy kingdom work. Isn't that amazing? Our God, the one who is all and everything, invites us to be used by him. Our job is to simply follow him into these good plans.

This leads us to a few other questions. Questions that center on trust and desire. Do we trust God enough to allow him to use us? And do we desire his plan so much that we are willing to surrender our own?

"For I know the plans I have for you," says the LORD. (Jeremiah 29:11 NLT)

This is where we find Moses. He was full of questions and full of doubt. He was working out his trust and desire issues. Did he choose to obey? Let's learn from Moses so we can make wise choices as we follow the I AM into the work we are called to do.

PRACTICE REMINDER

If you haven't already today, add seven to ten unique and praiseworthy items to your gratitude journal on page 58.

Day 3
Moses Continues to Question

Read Exodus 4:1–12.

Moses asked, "What if they do not believe me or listen to me and say, 'The LORD did not appear to you'?" (Exodus 4:1). This is the third question Moses asked of the Lord.

1. Consider the first two questions Moses asked and how God answered them (3:11–15). Do you think his third question is legitimate? Why or why not? What do you think Moses is really concerned about?

2. God responds to Moses's question by giving him three signs. How do you think Moses felt as he participated in each of these signs?

    Exodus 4:2–5

    Exodus 4:6–7

Exodus 4:9

3. What does God say are the reasons for the signs (4:5, 8)? How do you think this made Moses feel about his assignment from God?

"The Egyptians regarded the Nile River as the source of life and productivity. So Moses' showing the people that he had power over the Nile would prove that God had given Moses ability to overcome the Egyptians."

—John D. Hannah[1]

4. God was gracious and compassionate to give Moses these signs as proof of his calling. Chances are you've never experienced anything quite like the signs Moses was given. But God still shows himself miraculously active in our lives today. Have you ever observed or experienced a "sign" that helped you believe something about God or what he was asking you to do? If so, describe the situation and how it encouraged you.

5. Moses now brings up a concern. Fill out the chart below writing Moses's concern and God's response to him in your own words (verses 10–12).

Moses's Concern	God's Response

Some speculate Moses could have had real speaking issues (for example, stuttering). Others think it could be the language barrier due to the fact that he had not spoken the Egyptian language for forty years. Finally, others think he was just insecure (based on Acts 7:22). It's hard to say what the issue was. But the real concern was obedience. Would Moses move forward trusting God or not?

Now think through your own life. Do you have a concern or worry you think could get in the way of your usefulness to God? Write it and what you think God would say about it in the space below.

My Concern	I Think God Would Say

6. Have you ever felt called to do something that was out of your comfort zone and/or expertise? Describe the situation. What did you do? How did it make you feel? What did you learn about God?

PRACTICE REMINDER

If you haven't already today, add seven to ten unique and praiseworthy items to your gratitude journal on page 58.

Day 4
A Final Request

Read Exodus 4:13–17.

7. Moses has one final request for God. What does he request and how does God respond (Exodus 4:13–14)? Why do you think Moses's request incites this response from God? What do you think Moses was really saying?

8. Look up the following verses and fill in the chart to see how God responds to other requests in Scripture.

Scripture Passage	Speaker	Request	Response	Reaction or Result
2 Corinthians 12:7–10	Paul			(Consider verses 9–10)
Matthew 26:39, 42, 44	Jesus	*(Note: the cup is referring to Christ's coming suffering on the cross)*	Jesus dies on the cross, so the cup was not taken from him.	(Consider John 11:25)
Psalm 13	David		*We do not see a direct response from God.*	(Consider verses 5–6)

How does the heart attitude in the requests from the chart above differ from or correspond with the request Moses made in Exodus 4:13? How does this encourage or discourage you when you have questions for God?

9. Do you think our questions ever make God angry? What does this passage teach you about God's anger? How is this different from how we often experience human anger?

10. Have you ever made the decision not to do something you felt God was asking you to do? Describe the situation and why you chose to respond the way you did. What did you learn about yourself and God from this experience? If you were confronted with the same situation again, what would you do differently?

※

This encounter between God and Moses is a beautiful example of grace. Moses walked right up to the line of disobedience and potentially even crossed it. And God, in his grace, gave Moses what he did not deserve. Instead of continued anger or telling Moses no, God patiently met Moses where he was and gave him his brother Aaron as a helper. —Jodie

PRACTICE REMINDER

If you haven't already today, add seven to ten unique and praiseworthy items to your gratitude journal on page 58.

Day 5
Confirming the Calling

Read Exodus 4:18–31.

Moses interacts with three people (or groups of people) regarding the calling he has received from God. Look up each verse and write who these people are and how they react to Moses and the plan.

Verse	Who Moses Interacts With	Their Reaction
Exodus 4:18		
Exodus 4:27–30		
Exodus 4:29–31		

11. God often uses people to confirm a calling we have received from him. Has God ever used someone to do this in your life? If so, what happened and how did it encourage you?

12. God tells Moses, "When you return to Egypt, see that you perform before Pharaoh all the wonders I have given you the power to do" (Exodus 4:21). How does God say Pharaoh will react? Why do you think God tells Moses this?

13. According to verse 21, the Lord hardens Pharaoh's heart. Why does the Lord do this (see also 7:3–5)?

Many theologians are perplexed by Exodus 4:24–26. It seems strange that God would possibly kill Moses after all they had been through. One possible explanation is that Moses was acting in direct disobedience to God by not setting his son apart with circumcision as the Abrahamic covenant required (Genesis 17:1–14). This covenant was a bilateral agreement between God and man—meaning each would do something based on what the other did. If Moses did not comply with what he was supposed to do, then God would take action, which is potentially what was happening here. It was essential for Moses to be in compliance with the covenant in order to fulfill his calling.

This isn't something we need to worry about today, though. Because of Jesus's death and resurrection, we live under the new covenant

We will spend some more time exploring the question of who really hardens Pharaoh's heart—Pharaoh or God—in week 5. If you want to do some research now, try a trusted website like Bible.org to start your search on this challenging topic.

(Jeremiah 31:31–33; Matthew 5:17; Luke 22:19–20). This new covenant is a unilateral agreement from God and is not based on works or things we do to try to earn God's favor; instead, it is based solely on our faith in Jesus (Ephesians 2:8–9; Hebrews 9:15). Therefore, while we can't be certain why God was responding this way to Moses, we do know he will never respond this way to us. However, we should still live in obedience to the Lord out of a heart of gratitude for what he has done for us and how he paid the penalty for our sins through his own death.

14. How do the Israelites respond to Moses and Aaron, and what did this lead them to do (Exodus 4:31)?

15. The Israelites had been in slavery for nearly four hundred years. In this moment, God uses Moses to let them know he sees them and he has plans to rescue them. Have you ever had an experience where you felt hopeless and God used someone to remind you that you were seen and loved? If so, what happened?

16. Pause and ask God who you can encourage in their faith journey. If he brings someone to mind, make a plan to encourage them by the end of the day. If you don't feel like he brings a specific person to mind, then choose someone close to you. Your encouragement could be as simple as saying a prayer and sending a text or quick note to let them know you are praying for them. Feel free to be creative, but

choose something you can do before the end of the day. Write what you did and what happened.

Since we finished this lesson by encouraging others, I want to take a moment to encourage you. When God calls you to follow him, he will give you everything you need to do the work he's inviting you to. And, just like Moses, he will be with you every step of the way. So go ahead and ask the questions, but then boldly move forward knowing he won't let you down. Choose to follow the call; it's always worth it.

We have lots more to learn from Moses. Keep up the good work.

PRACTICE REFLECTION

As you worked on your gratitude journal this week, how did it impact you? Did it increase your trust in God? If so, how might this deeper trust help you follow God the next time he calls you to do something?

DEALING WITH DISCOURAGEMENT

Day 1
Practice—Social Media Fast

This week we will study how Moses deals with some significant discouragement. God forewarned Moses that the journey to set Israel free wouldn't be easy (Exodus 3:19–20; 4:21). And yet a theoretical awareness of hard times coming and the actual experience of walking through these hard times are two very different things. The real-life experience can quickly lead to discouragement.

For Moses, it started when the pharaoh, who he probably grew up with, harshly rejected him. And it was compounded when the Israelites, who he had come to help, turned against him. I can hardly blame Moses for feeling discouraged.

Discouragement can come in an instant through harsh words spoken to us or hard circumstances that come upon us. And it seems to settle in when we start doubting the goodness of God. We begin to wonder if his plans really are best, if things will ever get better, or if relief will ever come. And then discouragement really takes root when we allow the voices of the world to consistently drown out the promises of God.

The world speaks into our lives in a thousand different ways. Whether through social media, the latest movie, the endless news cycle, a coworker, or a friend, each can point us toward or away from the truth of Jesus. And while some of these voices are positive and needed, many of these voices pull us into a place of discouragement.

This week I want to invite you to fast from one voice that often leads us toward discouragement—social media. Studies show that social media often breeds social comparison which leads to general dissatisfaction and discouragement. This doesn't mean there aren't some really positive things about social media. For example, when I found myself in a season where I was unable to connect with friends face-to-face, I can't imagine how much harder it would have been without being able to connect through social media, but I also found that too much scrolling led me to a negative place. Even good tools need to be thoughtfully engaged.

This week, I want to invite you to see how social media impacts your heart and mind by fasting from it. If you don't regularly engage with social media, prayerfully ask the Lord what other media you could give up during this time. You might consider giving up the nightly news or whatever you listen to while you're driving.

As with any fast, the intention is to replace the thing you are fasting from with God. So perhaps each time you reach for your phone to check social media, you instead take a minute to pray or read a few verses of Scripture. This will help you stop passively filling your mind with things that could lead to discouragement and instead help you actively fill your mind with the truth of God. Win-win.

Think through your coming week. What will this fast look like for you? Make a plan and do your best to stick to it. If you slip up and break your fast inadvertently, don't get discouraged. Remember, we're trying to combat discouragement. So if that happens, give yourself grace and start again. The ultimate goal is to help us focus on God and allow his truths to be front and center in our minds instead of the world's lies.

I pray the Lord encourages you with his truths this week.

Make a note below of what social media you plan to fast from this week.

Day 2
Preparation

Read Exodus 5:1–6:13.

> *As you read this passage, write down anything that stands out to you along with any questions you may have.*

The first brave step of obedience in following God's leading can certainly be hard. It often feels a little like jumping off a cliff—exhilarating and scary all at the same time. But then we move into the endurance phase of obedience. And it's here, in taking the next step, and the next step, and the next step, that we can start to feel discouraged. These continual steps of obedience feel difficult because the newness has worn off and the excitement has died down. It's here in these longer journeys that we begin to wonder if there will be any real results, if we heard God correctly, or if maybe we're just delusional.

I felt this way in seminary. It took me six years to complete a two-year degree. I intentionally chose to go slow to honor other responsibilities, but that meant I lived for six years under piles of readings and deadlines. It never let up. And as the journey stretched on and on, I began to wonder why I was even doing this and if I had even heard God right in the first place. I battled some significant discouragement . . . and exhaustion.

Moses also faced significant discouragement in his calling. God told Moses what to do and even warned him that there would be trouble ahead. But as is often the case, God didn't give Moses many details. Moses boldly took the first step of obedience and confronted the pharaoh. It didn't go well. In fact, it went so poorly that it created more trouble and hardship for the Israelites. Then they turned against Moses too. No one was happy Moses had returned. I can't say what Moses was thinking in that moment, but if I were Moses I'd be thinking, *Really, God? I did exactly what you asked and no one has been rescued. In fact, their situation is ten times worse. At least before all this, everybody blamed the Egyptians for their suffering. Now everybody blames me! This is your great rescue plan?*

How did Moses fight against this discouragement? Did he throw up his hands and walk away, like I would be tempted to do? Or did he persevere without a second glance back? He actually did neither. I'm grateful to Moses for showing us how to persevere when circumstances become incredibly hard. And for teaching us how we can stay the course. Discouragement doesn't need to derail us. Let's learn from Moses so we can move through our discouragement and remain steadfast in our calling.

PRACTICE REMINDER

How are you doing with your media fast this week? If you've found yourself struggling to hold to it, make a plan for how you can commit to the fast for today.

Day 3
Discouraging Reactions

Read Exodus 5:1–21.

Exodus 4 ends with the Israelites worshipping God as they believed that Moses and his brother Aaron had been sent to rescue them. The nation of Israel seemed ready to do what they needed to do. Chapter 5 begins with Moses telling the pharaoh what would happen.

1. Moses and Aaron deliver the message to Pharaoh in Exodus 5:1–5. Write the conversation in your own words below.

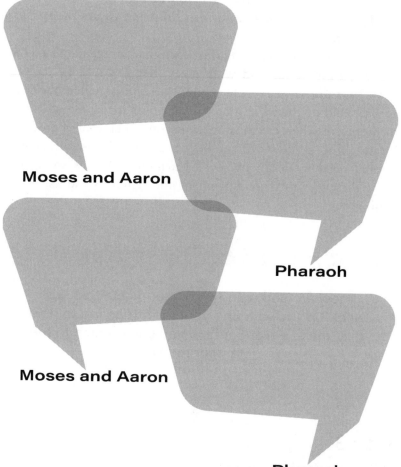

Moses and Aaron

Pharaoh

Moses and Aaron

Pharaoh

2. It's presumable that Moses and the pharaoh knew each other well; in fact many historians and theologians believe they were raised as brothers for forty years. Assuming this is true, how do you think each of the following people felt at this first meeting?

Moses

Pharaoh

Aaron

3. We tend to shorten Moses's phrase to, "Let my people go."
   What else does he say in 5:1 and 5:3? In that day, if an Israelite was participating in a festival or offering a sacrifice,
   what do you think they were doing in relationship to the
   Lord? Why do you think it's important to not forget this
   second part?

4. The pharaoh isn't interested in letting the Israelites leave
   to worship a God he does not know. What seems to be his
   primary motivation for keeping the Israelites where they
   are (verses 4–5)? What do you think this says about the
   pharaoh's values?

The pharaoh of Moses's youth tried to kill the Israelites
(Exodus 1:10, 16, 22) because he feared them and viewed them
as disposable. Now this pharaoh views them as an indispens-
able commodity. Neither ruler valued the Israelites as people.
I love that God values them and views them as his children
(4:22–23). He looks at us the same way. —Jodie

5. Not only does the pharaoh say no, but he also immediately
   increases the Israelites' workload to an unrealistic level
   (5:6–9). Why do you think he asks for something he knows
   is impossible? What is he hoping to accomplish?

After their workload is increased, the Israelite overseers boldly
appeal directly to the pharaoh to decrease their workload.
Pharaoh exhibits his hard heart (4:21) and stands firm in his original edict, holding the Israelites to an unrealistic workload (5:15–19).

The Israelite overseers, who
were like foremen, were slaves
yet had direct access to the
pharaoh. History tells us
these Egyptian slaves were
sometimes able to bypass
normal chains of command
and petition the pharaoh
directly. However, even when
they were able to make these
direct requests, most were not
granted.[1]

6. Read 5:20–21. Write what the
overseers say to Moses and Aaron
in your own words. What do you
think the overseers could have been
thinking and feeling as they said
these things to Moses and Aaron?

7. How do you think Moses felt about this?

8. The Israelites seem caught off guard by Pharaoh's decision not to let them leave to worship God in the wilderness. However, Exodus 4:30–31 says they had been told and seen everything God told and showed Moses. Review what the Israelites had been told as found in 3:18–22 and 4:21–23. How do you think the Israelites interpreted these words from God? Do you think they expected Pharaoh's hard heart to impact them? Why or why not?

9. Have you ever been called into a season of life you knew was going to be hard before you fully entered into it (health, relational, career, financial, etc.)? What was your attitude at the beginning of the hard season? What was your attitude once you fully entered into the season? If there was a change, why do you think it happened?

10. Discouragement comes from many places. In this case, the pharaoh and the Israelites are the primary drivers of discouragement for Moses. Who or what is currently discouraging you as you seek to follow God and his call on your life? Describe why it feels discouraging.

How are you doing with your media fast this week? If you've found yourself struggling to hold to it, make a plan for how you can commit to the fast for today.

Day 4
Handling Discouragement
Read Exodus 5:22–6:8.

11. What's the first thing we see Moses do after the Israelites talked to him (Exodus 5:22–23)? What do you think his tone of voice was? Do you think it was acceptable for Moses to question God in this way? Why or why not?

12. Think about a recent time you were discouraged regarding something you were pretty certain you were supposed to do. What was the first thing you did? Did it help? Explain why.

13. While we can't be sure of Moses's tone of voice or his heart attitude based on these verses, we do know he went to the Lord first to handle this situation. When do you tend to go to the Lord with your discouragement? Why is this?

14. God starts his response to Moses in 6:1. How do his words compare to what he says in 3:18–20? What do you think God is doing for Moses in this moment?

15. God continues his response in 6:2–8. He reminds Moses that he is the I AM and then tells Moses what he is to say to the Israelites. In the verses below, circle each time the Lord says "I will." What does this teach, tell, or remind you about God?

"Therefore, say to the Israelites: 'I am the LORD, and I will bring you out from under the yoke of the Egyptians. I will free you from being slaves to them, and I will redeem you with an outstretched arm and with mighty acts of judgment. I will take you as my own people, and I will be your God. Then you will know that I am the LORD your

God, who brought you out from under the yoke of the Egyptians. And I will bring you to the land I swore with uplifted hand to give to Abraham, to Isaac and to Jacob. I will give it to you as a possession. I am the LORD.'" (Exodus 6:6–8)

❊

"God's redeeming them *with an outstretched arm* (v. 6, emphasis added) meant that His power would be evident (cf. Deut. 4:34; 5:15; 7:19; 11:2; Ps. 136:12; Ezek. 20:33). And the *uplifted hand* (Ex. 6:8) was a gesture used when making an oath (as it still is today)."

—John D. Hannah[2]

16. Which "I will" statement means the most to you personally? Write it below:

   I will _____.

17. If you are facing discouragement right now, ask the Lord to remind you of a truth from his Word. (Here are some passages to start with: Joshua 1:9; Psalms 23; 46:1–3; Matthew 11:28; John 16:33.)

Once you've found a truth for your circumstance, take a few minutes to prayerfully personalize this word of encouragement as an "I will" statement from the Lord. (For example: I will give you courage and strength.) Consider writing down this word of encouragement and putting it where you will see it and can return to it whenever discouragement feels like it is coming upon you.

   I will _____.

If you need help finding a Scripture passage that speaks truth into your situation, try using Google. I've found it is actually a great tool for helping with this. You can type "scripture" or "bible verse" and then whatever the topic is, and usually something will come up that's helpful. A few words of caution when you do this, though. First, always check the source. There are a lot of great sources out there and unfortunately there are a lot of misinformed sources too. Make sure the sources you use are credible. You can do this by checking their belief statement or seeing if they are associated with a reputable Christian seminary or church. Second, check the context. Read the verses that surround the one that comes up to make sure it really speaks to what you are dealing with. A misused Scripture passage can prove almost anything. Be wise and prayerful. And ask a trusted friend who is further along in the journey if you need more help.

PRACTICE REMINDER

How are you doing with your media fast this week? If you've found yourself struggling to hold to it, make a plan for how you can commit to the fast for today.

Day 5
Falling Back on Fear

Read Exodus 6:9–13.

18. Moses obeys and reports God's word to the Israelites. How do they respond and why (Exodus 6:9)? If you were

one of those Israelites, how do you think that you would respond?

19. God also tells Moses to go back to the pharaoh and tell him to let the Israelites go. How does Moses reply to God (verses 10–12)? How does this compare to 4:10?

20. Do you tend to return to certain inadequacies and fears when you get discouraged? If so, what are they? Why do you think you do this?

If you are willing, share these things with your group as your prayer request for next week. If you don't want to share, consider inviting a close friend to speak truth into these perceived inadequacies and fears. Ask God to give you his perspective about these things.

21. God does not give up on Moses. Instead, verse 13 tells us he "commanded" him to move forward with his calling. Do you believe God wants you to move forward through

discouragement with something he is calling you to do? If so, what practical steps can you take this week?

22. Look back over this lesson. What have you learned about discouragement from Moses? Write down at least one thing you want to try next time you are discouraged in something God is calling you to.

Perhaps Moses still has a lot to learn. The desert taught him much, but experience can teach him more. He must learn to be still, and wait on God, relying wholly on the sovereign purpose of God which will ensure that the redemption of his people will take place.

—Iain D. Campbell[3]

Way to go! You just finished week 4 and your social media fast. Maybe you can survive without social media? It doesn't mean you have to, though. As you bring any media you fasted from back into your life, intentionally notice its impact on you. If it starts distracting your mind and heart away from God and his purposes for you, consider setting it aside again. God's plan is always worth the effort. Don't let the voices of our world consume you and discourage you from following him. Keep up the good work! I'm cheering you on.

PRACTICE REFLECTION

1. What did you choose to fast from this week? How did it go?

2. How did this activity encourage you or discourage you?

3. Did you learn anything new about God or yourself through this activity? If so, what?

FROM CRISIS OF FAITH TO FAITHFUL OBEDIENCE

Day 1
Practice—Listening to God

Moses was intentional about listening to God. He had the benefit of an audible voice, but he still had to be available and ready to listen to what God was telling him. Jesus was also intentional about listening to God. Scripture tells us he often retreated to "lonely places" to pray (Luke 5:16). These would have been quiet places to hear from God without distractions. If Moses and Jesus were intentional about listening to God, how much more do we need to be?

The challenge for many of us is getting quiet and still enough to actually hear God's voice. His voice is often referred to as a "gentle whisper" (see 1 Kings 19:11–12). And while God can absolutely get our attention in loud and large gestures, most find he whispers into their hearts when they are still long enough to hear him.

This week we are going to practice being still and silent in the

Lord's presence as a way to create space for listening to God. While it would be wonderful if he chose to speak to us in this quiet place, our agenda is to simply be in his presence without our words and thoughts driving the conversation. If we try to use stillness as a way to get God to speak to us, we've missed the point. We don't and can't control God. We simply create space so we are ready to listen when he is ready to speak. And until he speaks, we can rest in and enjoy his loving presence. As Psalm 46:10 tells us, it is enough to just "be still, and know that [he is] God."

To do this I recommend you find a quiet and peaceful place in your home. Once each day, sit in a comfortable yet attentive position, so you don't accidently fall asleep. And then set a timer for five minutes. Start with a few deep breaths and maybe say a short verse a few times over to calm your mind and keep it from wandering. Sit in stillness and silence, without talking to God, until the timer goes off.

Allow me to give you one quick warning before you start this activity. If you haven't done something like this before, you may be surprised by the random thoughts that come into your mind. Author James Bryan Smith describes these as "thought monkeys."[1] I think you will find this a very apt description. Try not to get frustrated by these random, I-haven't-thought-about-that-for-years thoughts. Either let them go or jot them down. Some find it helpful to recite a verse slowly as a way to refocus yourself on stillness in God's presence. I've found the words of Psalm 46:10, "Be still, and know that I am God," helpful. I say them slowly as I'm settling my mind and focusing on being present with him. And then I return to some or all of the words when the "thought monkeys" descend upon me.

In the end, the goal isn't emptying our minds. The goal is attuning our minds to God and being still in his loving presence. Hopefully you will find this practice helpful in refining your listening skills so that you can be more receptive to his still, small voice. When God is ready to speak to you, he will. Your job is to be ready to listen.

Day 2
Preparation

Read Exodus 6:28–7:13.

> *As you read this passage, write down anything that stands out to you along with any questions you may have.*

The very word *obedience* feels hard, doesn't it? After all, it means submitting to another's authority and doing what they wish instead of what we want. Even when we are talking about God, our good and trusted Father, it still means surrendering our will to his. Obedience is rarely easy.

I'm wrestling with obedience right now. I feel like God is asking me to reach out to my neighbor and I don't really want to. It's not that I don't care about my neighbor, but I know it will take time and I'm feeling short on time at the moment. I have a ton of work to get done including some deadlines I really can't miss. I've been letting his words weigh on me for the last few days. My lack of obedience is actually kind of ridiculous. He's asking me to do something that is pretty small. And yet, I find myself digging in and justifying why I don't need to do it and why it isn't that big of a deal. The problem is, I know God has placed this on my heart and therefore it is a big deal. Any time God asks us to do something, we need to do it. And any time we resist him, it's sin. And sin is always a big deal. So, yes, I will choose to walk in faith and reach out to my neighbor today. Especially since I've brought you into this for some added accountability. Here's the thing, I know obedience is always best. It does take time and sometimes it feels risky. But if God is inviting us into something, we are always wise to lay aside our own agenda and follow his lead.

Moses had this choice to make too. Would he live according to his own desires or surrender by faith to God's? Hebrews 11:24–28 tells us Moses made the choice to live by faith. He consistently chose to walk in faithful obedience to the Lord, even at great cost to himself. I doubt it ever got easy. But each time he surrendered to God's plan, he got to see the Lord show up and be faithful. Each and every time. And because Moses chose to walk in faithful obedience, he chose to live a life that truly mattered.

So what will you choose? I hope this week's lesson gives you some practical tools and encouragement for choosing to live by faith and walk in obedience.

PRACTICE REMINDER

If you haven't already, take five minutes to do our practice of sitting in stillness and silence before God. Don't forget to set a timer to help you manage the time.

Day 3
Crisis of Faith

Read Exodus 6:28–7:7.

In last week's lesson, we saw that Moses modeled both healthy and unhealthy ways to deal with discouragement. On the healthy side, we saw him go to God with his concerns (Exodus 5:22; 6:12). But on the unhealthy side, we saw him blame God for the problems (5:23) and worry about his inadequacies and fears (6:12, 30). The good news is that God received all of Moses's words and worries with patience and persistence.

Then God spoke words over Moses that seemed to help him turn the corner from discouragement and hesitancy toward consistently walking in faithful obedience.

1. Moses returns a third time to his insecurity about his poor speaking ability (6:12 and now again in v. 30). How does God respond to Moses (7:1–2)? Does God address Moses's insecurity directly? Why do you think this is?

2. In Exodus 7:1–2, what does God say are the roles of Moses and Aaron?

   Moses's role:

   Aaron's role:

> Prophets were appointed by God to speak on his behalf. The calling of prophet was a serious one. They were to speak only what the Lord told them to say, and if they added anything to the message claiming it was from God, or if they spoke on behalf of a false god, they were to be put to death (Deuteronomy 18:20).
> —Jodie

3. After their roles were reestablished, God answered Moses's question from Exodus 6:30, "Since I speak with faltering lips, why would Pharaoh listen to me?" Why does God say the pharaoh *won't* listen (7:3)? How does God ultimately answer Moses's concern in 7:4?

> I find it almost comical that God answers Moses's fear-based question, "Why would the pharaoh listen to me?" with, "He won't." What if God answered me like this? Would I have the courage to move ahead? I hope so. Because the bottom line is, it's not about Moses and it's not about me. It's about God and what he's doing. —Jodie

How do you think Moses might have felt about this response from God?

4. Look up a few of the times Pharaoh's heart is said to be hard in Exodus 7–11 (7:3, 14; 8:15, 19, 32; 9:7, 12, 34–35; 10:1, 20, 27; 11:10).

What do you notice about who hardens Pharaoh's heart each time?

The question of who hardened Pharaoh's heart is a tough one. To help us understand the answer we need to hold two truths in tension. The first is that God gives every person the freedom and ability to choose whether or not they will live a life surrendered to him. The second is that he is sovereign (see definition in sidebar) and will ensure that his will is ultimately done. This leads us to the answer that both Pharaoh and God hardened Pharaoh's heart. Pharaoh, who is rebellious to the core, repeatedly resisted God. God, in his grace, gave him chance after chance to repent and choose obedience until, finally, God, in his solemn, sovereign judgment, left Pharaoh alone. And in this act,

"SOVEREIGNTY OF GOD: Biblical teaching that God possesses all power and is the ruler of all things (Ps. 135:6; Dan. 4:34–35). God rules and works according to His eternal purpose, even through events that seem to contradict or oppose His rule."[2]

Pharaoh's sinfulness and rebellion took over and his heart was fully and finally hardened.

5. According to Exodus 7:6, Moses and Aaron do just what the Lord told them to do. Why do you think Moses obeys God at this point? What do you think has happened in his heart regarding his questions, concerns, and discouragement? Do you think he ever struggled again with these things?

"What is noticeable is that there is no reference to God's hardening the heart of Pharaoh until after the sixth plague is well under way. . . . Pharaoh, at least once more, can harden his own heart. . . . But after that God, and God alone, does the hardening. . . . It is as if Pharaoh's window of opportunity has slammed shut."

—Victor P. Hamilton[3]

6. Are you hesitant to choose to obey God in something he is asking you to do? If so, what questions or concerns do you have for God about what you think he is asking of you?

7. What do you think God wants to say to you in response to your questions? Pray and ask him. Then write an imaginary letter from God to you of what you think his response would be. (Remember as you do this imagination activity

that you need to weigh any words you feel like God might be saying to you with Scripture. God will never contradict his Word.) Is this the first time you think God has said this to you? Or has he said something like this to you multiple times like he did for Moses? If multiple times, why do you think you struggle to believe these words?

8. Based on your letter from question 7, what are some practical ways you can remind yourself of the truth of who God is, when circumstances, insecurities, fears, or anything else threatens to derail you from obeying him? Brainstorm some ideas (including Scriptures) to share with your group. After your group has shared, choose one idea to implement next time something threatens to derail you.

"By continually giving Pharaoh another chance, God is as long-suffering with Pharaoh as he was with Moses after the burning bush. Moses's repeated "I will not go" is matched by Pharaoh's repeated "I will not let you go." That God has to act ten times before Pharaoh acquiesced is neither unexpected nor surprising."

—Victor P. Hamilton[4]

PRACTICE REMINDER

If you haven't already, take five minutes to do our practice of sitting in stillness and silence before God. Don't forget to set a timer to help you manage the time.

Day 4
First Steps of Obedience

Read Exodus 7:8–13.

9. What is the first miracle Moses, through Aaron, performs for the pharaoh? Why do you think this is the miracle God had Moses do first (recall Exodus 4:1–5)?

How did the pharaoh respond (verses 11–13)? Where do you think the wise men, sorcerers, and Egyptian magicians got their power? Whose power was greater, God's or these men's? How do you know?

10. Imagine you are Moses going before a powerful pharaoh, performing the staff-to-snake miracle and then receiving the response Moses received. Fill in the chart on the next page with what you might be thinking and feeling each step of the way. Then reflect on and respond to how you think your faith would increase as a result of this entire incident.

Action	What I Might Be Thinking
Throwing down the staff	
Staff becomes a snake	
Pharaoh's summoned officials who replicate the miracle and multiple staffs become snakes	
Aaron's staff swallows up each of their staffs	

I think my faith would be increased because:

11. Think back to a time when you stepped out in obedience to do something you believed God was asking you to do. What happened? How did your faith in God increase or falter following this act of obedience?

※

The closer I am to God, the more I trust him. The more I trust him, the more I am willing to obey him. The more I obey him, the more I see his faithfulness. And in this process my faith grows stronger, which brings me closer to God. It's a positive cycle that God uses to help me grow. —Jodie

Not every act of obedience brings successful results as we define success. In fact, Moses experienced this multiple times. He went to the pharaoh to make his bold requests and kept getting turned down. It certainly seems like his obedience was often unsuccessful. I've had this happen in my own life too. For example, I told you earlier I was feeling led to reach out to my neighbor, which I did. I offered to help her with something she needed, but she turned me down. This certainly felt unsuccessful and left me wondering if I had heard God correctly. And then I remembered that I don't get to define what success looks like. I don't know what God is up to in my neighbor's life. I just need to be faithful to do what I sense God is asking me to do. Perhaps I'll never get to know why I was supposed to choose that act of obedience. That has to be OK. God is working even when we don't clearly see the results—or even when the results are the exact opposite of what we hoped they would be.

12. Now think back to a time when you resisted being obedient to God. How did you disobey him? What happened? Did this act of resistance or disobedience impact your faith? If so, how?

PRACTICE REMINDER

If you haven't already, take five minutes to do our practice of sitting in stillness and silence before God. Don't forget to set a timer to help you manage the time.

Day 5
Going and Growing—Consistent Obedience

Scan Exodus 7:14–11:10; 12:29–36.

These chapters detail the ten plagues that came upon Pharaoh and the Egyptians. As you scan these chapters, you will notice that these plagues may seem unnecessarily harsh. But their divine purpose was not cruel punishment—it was so Pharaoh and his people would turn away from their false gods and come to know the one true God. In fact, many theologians believe that each plague specifically addressed a false god the Egyptians worshipped. Either way, God explicitly told Pharaoh before the seventh plague, the plague of hail, that the purpose is for them to "know that there is no one like me in all the earth. For by now I could have stretched out my hand and struck you and your people with a plague that would have wiped you off the earth" (Exodus 9:14–15). But God didn't wipe Pharaoh and the Egyptians off the earth because he is patient. God desires everyone to know him and turn to him. Even the cruelest and harshest people on earth . . . like Pharaoh (2 Peter 3:9).

"The 10 plagues may have occurred over a period of about nine months. The 1st occurred when the Nile rises (July–August). . . . And the 10th plague (chaps. 11–12) occurred in April, the Passover month. By the plagues God was judging the gods of Egypt (of which there were many) and showing Himself superior to them."

—John D. Hannah[5]

13. Think back over your life. What are some ways God has revealed himself to you (circumstances, his Word, his people, answered prayers, etc.)? How do these things help you trust him more, especially as you seek to follow him in obedience?

We aren't going to study the plagues specifically, although they make for an interesting study. Instead, we will continue our focus on Moses and what happened between him and God as he executed each of these plagues and discover what we can learn from Moses as he walked this challenging road.

14. Exodus 7:14 says, "Then the LORD said to Moses." When God speaks to Moses, Moses listens. Think about a recent time when someone told you something important. What were some things you did to help you listen well? Do you think Moses had to do similar things? What do you think were Moses's responsibilities in this interaction with God?

15. Think about your part in hearing from God. What are some things you can do to help you better hear from him?

Do you need to make any changes in the way you are currently interacting with God? If so, think of one thing you can do this week to help foster this change and then make a plan to do it. Share it with your group for accountability.

⚘

Just because we position ourselves in expectation, waiting for God to speak, doesn't mean we will always hear something specific from him. Yes, God is always moving and present but we can't control when he speaks to our hearts in individual ways. We can only make ourselves ready to hear when he does. —Jodie

16. Skim through the plagues that begin with the following verses. Choose as many or as few of the following passages as you have time for: Exodus 7:14; 8:1, 16, 20; 9:1, 8, 13; 10:1, 21; and 11:1. What do you notice as the common theme that starts each plague? What do you think this says about the relationship between Moses and God?

17. Moses responds in a consistent way to what the Lord says to him. Skim the plagues again (do as many verses as you have time for), specifically focusing on the following verses: 7:6, 10, 20; 8:6, 17; 9:10, 23; 10:3, 22; and 11:4. What do you notice Moses does each time?

18. Moses also communicates back to God. How does he do this (8:12–13, 30–31; 9:33; 10:18–19)? Why do you think God answers these prayers? How does this encourage you?

Unlike Moses's prayers, a tragic example of people not praying according to God's will is found in James 4:3. This verse says the people's prayers were not answered because they were asking with self-serving motives to fulfill their sinful desires. While this is an example of how not to pray, there are many examples of prayers that God delights in answering. If you're interested in reading about some of these start with John 15:7–8, James 1:5, and 1 John 1:9.

19. Describe the "back-and-forth" relationship between God and Moses throughout chapters 7–12. What do you think happened to Moses's faith as a result?

20. Have you experienced this kind of back-and-forth relationship with God? If so, when was it and what was happening? What were the results of this period? If you haven't experienced a period of time like this, why do you think that is?

21. How has this lesson encouraged or challenged you in your relationship with God? Pray and ask God if there is anything he wants you to do so you can enter into or stay in a season of growth. Write what you think God is asking you to start doing or keep doing. Spend a few minutes praying and asking God to help you.

Remember, we can't do anything to earn God's forgiveness or love. We are forgiven only because of our faith in Jesus—not because of anything we do or don't do (Ephesians 2:8–9). This leads many to question why we even need to bother being obedient to God. The answer is we live obediently because we trust God and believe his plan is better than our own (John 14:15; Romans 12:1–2). Trust takes time to build though.

If you're struggling to follow God in obedience, don't forget it took Moses some time to start moving forward too. God was patient with Moses. As their relationship developed and Moses's fears were quieted, his trust in God grew. This made the difference. It's hard to obey someone you don't trust and trust is built in relationship. If you are wrestling with obedience, ask yourself if you really trust God with the area of your life you feel like he's asking you to surrender. If you don't trust him, why? This is the best place for you to start praying and asking God for help. Keep at it. It is a process. God will be patient with you just like he was with Moses.

PRACTICE REFLECTION

1. What was the practice of sitting in stillness and silence before God like for you? Would you describe it as hard, easy,
   or something else?

2. Did you notice anything new about God or yourself as a
   result of this activity? If so, what?

PREVENTING PRIDE

Day 1
Practice—Worship

It was a crummy day. If something could go wrong, it did. Work was hard. Relationships were hard. My body hurt. Even when I tried to sit down and spend some time with Jesus, my dogs went ballistic. I felt like they were overtaken by the enemy as one more attempt to send me careening over the edge. It almost worked. And all before nine in the morning.

With my morning off to an abysmal start, I gathered my things and headed to work. My radio was already set to the news, so as I pulled out of my driveway, my discouragement was compounded by the news of how awful the world was acting. Ugh. It just wouldn't seem to stop.

To escape the news I switched to some worship music. I listened at first and then couldn't help but start to sing along. As I echoed the words of the songs, my soul was reminded of God's truth. The woe-is-me cycle began to fade away and I started to regain perspective. God was still God. He was still very much in control. The hard was still hard, but I was not alone. He was with me—strengthening me, holding me, reminding me. It was just what I needed to refocus myself so I could face the rest of the day.

Moses also faced a lot of hard days. He could have easily allowed his common sense, his efforts, or even the approval of others to derail him. Yet somehow he stayed focused on God. He didn't have the same worship music we have, but he did worship. And I'm certain that as he intentionally reminded himself of truth, it also helped him not get caught in his own woe-is-me cycle.

This week we are going to practice refocusing ourselves on God through intentionally engaging in worship through music. There are two parts to our practice this week. First, take five minutes a day to deliberately worship God through music. Second, attend all of Sunday worship at your church. This means you need to make a plan to arrive a few minutes early so you can take advantage of the entire worship time. If for some reason you can't be physically present at church this week and you are attending online, then make sure you are logged on and ready to go early. Also, if you are physically able, stand for the worship time to try to be as engaged as you can. As you listen during the week and worship with your church on the weekend, try to be fully present with God and allow his truth to go deep into your heart and soul.

If you aren't sure what to listen to, try typing "favorite worship songs of all time" into an internet search engine. You can usually play the songs right from there. My favorites change depending on the season I'm in, but some of my go-to worship songs are "Blessed Be Your Name" by Matt Redman, "Come, Thou Fount of Every Blessing" by Chris Rice, "Do it Again" by Elevation Worship, and "New Wine" by Hillsong Worship.

Day 2
Preparation

Read Exodus 13:17–14:31.

As you read this passage, write down anything that stands out to you along with any questions you may have.

In the previous lesson we skimmed the ten plagues. The last plague was the breaking point for Pharaoh. This plague, the plague of death, included both people and animals. Only those who showed they feared and believed in the Lord by putting the blood of a perfect year-old lamb over their doors would be exempt. The blood of this lamb was a signal for the Lord to "pass over" or protect that house from death. After this tenth plague of death, Pharaoh, whose own son was killed, relented and in his anguish sent the Israelites

This act of God passing over and thus saving his people is remembered and celebrated as the Passover. The original Passover is rich with symbolism that points to Jesus and his death on the cross. Jesus is the true perfect Lamb and it is his blood that covers over and protects us from ultimate death (John 1:29; 1 Corinthians 5:7). —Jodie

away. This began the next part of a difficult journey, for both Moses and the Israelites.

As I've been studying Moses, I've wondered what enacting all these plagues must have been like for him and Aaron. Repeatedly Moses or Aaron would do or say something that would result in a plague coming upon the land and the people. Then Pharaoh would beg Moses for relief and make false promises. And each time Moses would pray and immediately God would respond and end the destruction. Again and again this pattern cycled with different perils and infestations. I imagine that parts of this experience were exhilarating for Moses. After all, that's a lot of power. It would be dangerously easy to let this kind of power go to your head. Moses could have thought, "You think frogs are bad, check out these boils." Pride could quickly set in. If it was me, I might start to think I was the one in control instead of God.

On the other hand, Moses and Aaron's burden was somber and heavy to carry. Death, destruction, pain, and suffering were ushered in through their hands and words and out through Moses's prayers. Power like this could crush someone. Again, if it was me, I might hide in a corner and cry, begging God to find someone else and refusing to go any further.

It's interesting to me that both of my potential reactions center around pride. I seem to think that either I would let the power go to my head or I would refuse to go further. Sadly, both extreme reactions are focused on me. Pride is sneaky. It creeps up on us when we least expect it. We may start out in full dependence upon the Lord, but then somewhere along the way we get a little distracted and start to drift away. Subtly we start to depend more on ourselves and less on God. And this can lead us straight into the pit of pride. It takes diligence to fight against it. Thankfully Moses shows us that to fight against pride we must stay close to God. It was never about Moses or Aaron. It was always about God, his power, and what he was accomplishing.

This week we will observe how Moses avoided three potential pride pitfalls and remained faithful as he followed God.

It couldn't have been easy, but his life gives us some good practical tools for how we can manage similar scenarios.

PRACTICE REMINDER

Take a few minutes to intentionally worship God through listening to and engaging with worship music, if you haven't already.

Day 3
Pride Pitfall 1: Thinking We Know Better Than God

Read Exodus 13:17–22.

1. Look at the map below. Three potential routes from Egypt to the land God promised to the Israelites' forefathers are noted on the map. Mark the route you would probably choose to lead the people from Rameses (in Egypt) to the promised land. (We will use Mount Nebo as the point

where the promised land begins because Deuteronomy 34:1 says that Moses viewed the promised land from this point.)

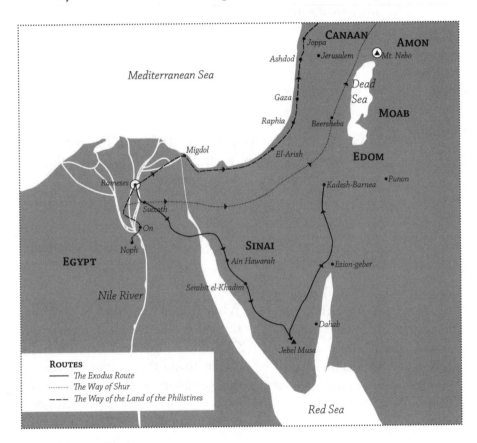

2. According to Exodus 13:17, which route did God not allow them to take? Why? How do you think Moses felt about this? How do you think the people reacted to going in a direction that didn't make sense to them?

3. Have you ever felt like God was asking you to follow him in a direction that didn't make sense? What happened? Did the journey make sense in hindsight? Why or why not?

4. Is God currently asking you to do something that seems counterintuitive? If so, what are your fears with following what you think he is asking you to do?

Exodus 12:37 tells us that there were "six hundred thousand men on foot, besides women and children." Most scholars believe this means there were upwards of 2 million people who made up the massive exodus caravan.

....

While Moses was asked to do something that didn't seem to make sense, God doesn't always or even usually ask us to do things that go against our common sense. Remember, he gave us the ability to make good decisions and unless he tells us otherwise, he expects us to make the best decisions we can. However, he also sees things we don't, and it's always in our best interest to continually ask him how he wants us to proceed. Sometimes what looks like the long or hard way is actually the best route.

5. Read Isaiah 55:8–9. What specifically do these verses say about God's ways as compared to our ways? Does this encourage you to trust his ways over yours? Why or why not?

6. How was the Lord present with the people as they traveled? Did he ever leave them while they were on this journey (Exodus 13:21–22)?

How do you think this made the Israelites feel?

7. Read the following verses and consider what each says about how God is present with believers today.

Where can I go from your Spirit?
    Where can I flee from your presence?
If I go up to the heavens, you are there;
    if I make my bed in the depths, you are there.
If I rise on the wings of the dawn,
    if I settle on the far side of the sea,
even there your hand will guide me,
    your right hand will hold me fast.
    (Psalm 139:7–10)

And I will ask the Father, and he will give you another advocate to help you and be with you forever—the Spirit of truth. The world cannot accept him, because it neither sees him nor knows him. But you know him, for he lives with you and will be in you. (John 14:16–17)

Be satisfied with what you have. For God has said, "I will never fail you. I will never abandon you." (Hebrews 13:5 NLT)

According to these verses:

Will God ever leave us?

What is his role in our lives?

How does this encourage you to follow God even when it doesn't make sense?

To help the Israelites on their journey, God gave them his physical guiding presence as a cloud by day and fire by night. This ever-present leading was a grace to the weary travelers as it reminded them that God was with them and providing for them every step of the way. While we don't get to see a physical manifestation of God's guiding and leading for us today, we do have the gift of the Holy Spirit who is ever-present and faithfully leading us too. I most often hear the promptings of the Spirit when I'm praying, reading and reflecting on God's Word, and responding in love to the circumstances he places me in.

PRACTICE REMINDER

Take a few minutes to intentionally worship God through listening to and engaging with worship music, if you haven't already.

Day 4
Pride Pitfall 2: Taking Credit for God's Work

Skim Exodus 14.

8. The pharaoh's hard heart causes him to chase after the Israelites. How do the Israelites react to seeing Pharaoh and his army? Who do they blame for their predicament (14:10–12)?

9. What does Moses say to the people (14:13–14)? How do you think they reacted to these words as they saw the army bearing down on them?

The Israelites seemed to believe they only had two options: death at the hands of their enemy or surrender and return to a life of slavery. I think we do the same thing in our lives. When faced with a hard situation, we tend to believe our options are only the few outcomes we can clearly see. But often God has a plan that we've never even considered. He invites us to simply take the next step and trust him, even when we don't know exactly how things will turn out.

10. How does the Lord fight for his people? What role does Moses have in the saving of the Israelites (14:19–22)? What role do the Israelites have in being saved?

"And while it was God doing the saving, their salvation did require a response of faith. They had to put their faith in what God had said. Their faith became evident when they took that first step into the Red Sea."

—Nancy Guthrie[1]

11. Once the Israelites make it through the Red Sea, what does the Lord instruct Moses to do (14:26–29)? Perhaps you've heard this story many times before, but pause for a moment and consider what this must have been like. How do you think you would have felt if you had been there? How do you think Moses felt?

12. How many of the Israelites do you think saw Moses's part in this miracle? What does Exodus 14:31 say they did next? How do you think Moses felt about their response?

13. What could have happened if Moses allowed pride to take over and started to take some or all of the credit for what God did? How do you think the people could have started treating him?

14. Have you ever had an experience where you've been obedient to do something you felt the Lord asked you to do and it turned out well? Describe what happened and how you either did or did not struggle with taking credit for the work God did. What did you learn from this situation?

Moses is tied closely to the Lord at the end of chapter 14. Which, given the fickle faith of the Israelites, makes me wonder how long it will be before they try to make Moses a god and worship him too. Thankfully the song in chapter 15 is all about worshipping the Lord. Reading this song, rich with truth and humility, tells me that the Israelites were in a place of true faith and trust. This is a rare and beautiful moment where they get it right. It doesn't last though, which is frustrating, but real. I think the Israelites' faith journey is reflective of our lives. We have deep trust and faith some days and other days we wander away and rely on our own efforts.

15. What does the next verse say that Moses and the people do (15:1)? How do you think this impacted their hearts? How does singing to the Lord tend to impact your heart? Why do you think this is?

Day 5
Pride Pitfall 3: Seeking the Approval of Others

Read Exodus 15:22–26; 16:1–8; 17:1–6.

16. Read the following verses. Circle the words *grumbled* and *quarreled*.

The people grumbled against Moses, saying, "What are we to drink?" (15:24)

In the desert the whole community grumbled against Moses and Aaron. The Israelites said to them, "If only we had died by the LORD's hand in Egypt! There we sat around pots of meat and ate all the food we wanted, but you have brought us out into this desert to starve this entire assembly to death." (16:2–3)

So they quarreled with Moses and said, "Give us water to drink."

Moses replied, "Why do you quarrel with me? Why do you put the LORD to the test?"

But the people were thirsty for water there, and they grumbled against Moses. They said, "Why did you bring us up out of Egypt to make us and our children and live-stock die of thirst?" (17:2–3)

> Given all the experiences the people have been through (the plagues, crossing the Red Sea, God's constant presence as a pillar of cloud and fire, etc.), what do you think of their reaction?

17. If Moses got caught in the pitfall of trying to seek the approval of others, how do you think he could have reacted when the Israelites were angrily demanding food and water? How did Moses respond instead (15:25; 17:4)?

18. What did the Lord do about the grumbling (15:25; 16:4–5; 17:5–6)? What do you think this reveals about the character of God?

19. Read the definitions of *grace* below. How does God administer grace through Moses in these situations?

Grace defined: "Grace is God's free and unmerited favor shown to guilty sinners who deserve only judgment."

—Jerry Bridges[2]

"Grace means there is nothing I can do to make God love me more, and nothing I can do to make God love me less. It means that I, even I who deserve the exact opposite, am invited to take my place at the table in God's family."

—Philip Yancey[3]

20. Does Moses take the grumbling of the Israelites personally (16:8)? How do you think he is able to keep it in perspective? How do you think this helps him stay out of the pitfall of pridefully seeking the Israelites' approval?

21. Reflect on your last week. Think of a time where you either were tempted to or did seek the approval of others. Describe what happened and why you think you responded this way. What practical ideas can you take from Moses's example to help you the next time you are tempted in this way?

22. Is there someone in your life who grumbles and complains against you, even when you are trying your best to follow God? If so, pray and ask God how he might want you to hand this situation over to him and possibly even offer them grace. Write any ideas that come to mind. (As always, remember to weigh any ideas or thoughts against God's Word, as he will never contradict himself.)

Moses faced three distinct potential pride traps in this lesson: The temptation to think he knew better than God, the allure of taking credit for God's work, and the possible desire to seek the approval of others over God. Moses successfully navigated each of these potential pitfalls by turning to God and trusting him. We saw Moses make three really good choices, but don't be fooled—that doesn't mean it was easy for him.

You might be facing one of these potential pitfalls in your own life right now. If not today, it may be right around the corner. It could be something big or small, but it has the potential to throw you off course.

Let me encourage you to fight back against pride by turning to our practice and taking a few minutes to praise God and remember who he is through spending some time in worship. Don't let these pesky pitfalls win. Remember that God is with you, he fights for his people, and he is full of grace.

Let me also encourage you to keep at the hard work of this study. We've crossed the halfway point. Great job! Keep at it. We still have some really important truths to learn from Moses. If you've been struggling with setting aside time to study, ask God to help you figure out how to get back on track. You've got this. I know you can do it!

PRACTICE REFLECTION

1. Did you notice any changes in your thinking or emotions after your times of worship this week? If so, explain them. How might these changes help you combat pride in your life?

2. Was there a difference in worshipping alone versus worshipping in community? If so, what was it? How might both be valuable in your relationship with the Lord?

3. Was there any aspect of this practice that surprised you, encouraged you, or even discouraged you? If so, what was it?

REMEMBERING WELL

Day 1
Practice—Journaling

I was in the middle of telling a great story when one of my friends jumped in and with a mischievous smile said, "That's not how I remember it." She then proceeded to fill in some details I had missed and tell her version of how it happened. We went back and forth piecing the story together, correcting each other and having a few good laughs along the way.

As I reflected on this experience and many others like it, I wondered what happened. Why were some parts of our stories the same and other parts totally different and contradictory? Neither of us was lying, so that couldn't be the reason. The truth is our memories are fluid, malleable, and always changing. Research tells us that memories decay and get dulled as new memories are layered over the old ones. Studies also show that stress and multitasking are huge enemies to accurate memories.

This research helps me have a little more grace for my forgetfulness, but it doesn't give me a pass. I know I need to remember with more intentionality, especially when it comes to my faith journey. I need to be able to readily recall with accuracy God's past faithfulness so I can trust his leading in the future. The author of Psalm 77 exemplifies this for us. When he was faced with wondering about the future, he intentionally chose to recall how God had proven himself faithful in the past. He states, "I will remember the deeds of the LORD; yes, I will remember your miracles of long ago. I will consider all your works and meditate on all your mighty deeds" (verses 11–12).

So how can we do this? How can we strengthen our memory muscle especially when it comes to God's faithfulness to us? One way we can do this is through journaling. Research shows that writing down memories reinforces them and helps us hold on to them longer. I know this is true for me. I've also found that writing things down jogs my memory and helps me remember additional details. And as an added bonus, it provides a record I can go back to when I need some encouragement.

This week we are going to practice strengthening our memory muscle regarding God's faithfulness by journaling about an experience we've had or are having with God. To do this practice, set aside about thirty minutes sometime this week to prayerfully go through the journaling prompts provided below. As you do, remember this is for you and your memory. No one is going to check your grammar or sentence structure, and for sure no one is going to jump in and say, "That's not how I remember it." The goal is not a perfectly written story. The goal is an experience that helps you remember God's faithfulness.

May you be reminded that he has never let you down in the past and encouraged that he won't let you down in the future either.

Journaling Prompts

Pray and ask the Lord to help you recall a time in your life when he directed you in an unmistakable way. Jot down the ideas that come to mind and then choose one and respond to the following prompts.

What was going on in your life?

What direction did you believe you were hearing from God?

What circumstances, Scripture passages, people, or other occurrences helped confirm that this was God's leading for you?

What did you do as a result?

How did it feel?

What happened as a result of following God?

How did this experience affect your faith?

Is there something you should be doing today as a result of what you learned from this experience?

Day 2
Preparation

Read Exodus 16:2–3, 11–35; 17:8–16; Deuteronomy 8:7–18.

As you read these passages, write down anything that stands out to you along with any questions you may have.

Over the years, I've come to terms with the fact that I don't have the best memory. My family, friends, and coworkers have had to come to terms with it too. Sometimes it's the little things—like walking to the kitchen for something and having no idea what it was. Or forgetting to buy that one thing I went to the grocery store for. I botch names, birthdays, appointments, and meetings all because I just forgot. I know I'm not alone; you do it too. It's one of the telltale signs of living in a busy, distracted, and multitasking world.

What really bothers me, though, is when I forget the big things. I'll have a significant experience, either good or bad, and be certain I will never forget how it felt, what was said, or what it looked like. And then time moves on. The feelings level out and the memory begins to fade.

My memory may be worse than average, but we all struggle with remembering, to some extent. God knew this would be the case. He knew that even the Israelites, who witnessed their supernatural deliverance and exodus from Egypt, and who afterward experienced the Lord's miraculous daily provision for forty years, would eventually start to forget. He knew they would be tempted to rationalize the miraculous by explaining it away as their own logic and efforts—or even their good luck.

How could they forget after all they had seen? It's easy to judge them, until I take a look at myself.

I've experienced amazing answered prayers—miraculous interventions of God in my life that left me awed and astonished. Did God—the God of the universe—do that for me?

And then a few days slide by. I pause to reflect on what he did and start to wonder: Maybe that wasn't really God. Maybe it was just circumstances or serendipity or something else, but I'm not sure that was really God. Nothing has changed—an amazing work of God still happened—but my memory has started to dull, and as a result I start to rationalize away the miraculous.

God knows my mind well. He knows all our minds well. He knows our propensity to forget or even to take credit, and so he tells us to remember. We will see this as we study Moses this week.

God told Moses to remember by writing the stories down, verbally retelling these stories, and even collecting memorable objects to ensure they wouldn't forget. Why? Because God knows that remembering people are faithful people. I want to be a remembering person. Don't you? Let's observe and learn from God and Moses to see some ways we can better remember God's faithfulness in the past, so we can confidently choose to follow God wherever he is leading us in the future.

PRACTICE REMINDER

If you haven't done so already, set aside about thirty minutes sometime this week to prayerfully go through the journaling prompts in the practice section on pages 123–124.

Day 3
Physical Reminders

Read Exodus 16:2–3, 11–35.

As we read last week, after experiencing God's miraculous rescue from Egypt, the people of Israel entered a "desert" season of their journey. It didn't take long for them to start grumbling against

Moses because they were hungry. God, in his grace, met their needs and provided food. But as we will see, he does it with the hope that their faith will be built.

1. What kind of food does the Lord provide for the Israelites in the morning? What kind of food does he give them in the evening (Exodus 16:11–16, 31)? How does the Lord provide this food?

2. Of the two foods, which one is more familiar? What more can you learn about manna from Exodus 16:4, 14, and Numbers 11:7–8? Write down all the ways it is described. Does manna sound like any food you have ever had or seen? How would you feel if God provided this kind of food for you week after week?

I love that God uses both ordinary (quail) and extraordinary (manna) ways to provide for his people. He does the same for us. Unfortunately, we're prone to overlook or explain away some of these ordinary yet still miraculous provisions. Imagine if a quail crash-landed in your backyard just when it was time for dinner and the refrigerator was empty, and you thought, "Wow, what a coincidence!" Instead, we should be overwhelmed with gratitude to God who has just miraculously provided for our needs in an ordinary, yet extraordinary, way.

3. The Israelites were instructed to gather only enough manna for each day, except on the sixth day, when they were told to gather enough for two days. If they tried to store any manna overnight, except on the sixth day, what happened to it (16:19–20)? Why do you think this happened to the manna they kept? What might the Lord have been trying to teach them?

4. The Israelites only received enough bread for each day. If you were one of the Israelites, what do you think this would have been like?

Exodus 16:16 says each person was to gather an omer of manna. One omer is roughly equivalent to two quarts or eight cups.[1]

· · · · · · · ·

I think it was both hard and easy for the Israelites to trust in God's daily provision. They had been through so much and God had always been faithful. I'm guessing they woke up each morning and upon seeing the manna thought, "Of course, more manna." But I also imagine they struggled each night as they went to bed wondering if tomorrow would be the day he left them on their own. Yet he never left them on their own. He continued to prove himself faithful! He does the same for us.

5. In Exodus 16:32, what does Moses say God commands them to do with a portion of the manna? What do you

think the Lord intended in commanding them to keep some manna for future generations?

6. Has God ever clearly provided for you in a miraculous way during a tough season in your life? Is there an object you can find that would remind you of his provision? If so, what is it and why does it relate to the provision? Consider bringing this object, or a picture of it, to share with your small group.

"The Hebrew word, *man hu'* means 'what is it?' That's what they called this miraculous food that was sent to them by God every morning for forty years. For forty years the people ate 'what is it?' 'What's for supper?' someone would ask, and the answer was always 'what is it?' There was never anything like it before and hasn't been since."
—Nancy Guthrie[2]

7. Read John 6:26–51. Write down a few comparisons or contrasts between manna and Jesus. If you only eat manna, what will eventually happen to you? If you eat the true bread, Jesus, what will happen? How do you "eat" this true bread? How have you experienced the true bread sustaining you as you follow God's leading in your life?

God taught the Israelites daily dependence on him by providing what they needed one day at a time. Jesus invites us to have this same kind of dependence upon him by instructing us to pray, "Give us today our daily bread" (Matthew 6:11). There have been many seasons in my life where I've had to cling to this prayer as I sought God's provision (physically, mentally, or emotionally) to help me make it through the day. He has always been faithful to answer these prayers. If you find yourself in a tough season, lean on this prayer and then rest in some of Jesus's next words, "Do not worry about tomorrow, for tomorrow will worry about itself" (Matthew 6:34).

> "This bread was not a 'what is it?' but a 'who is it?' Jesus . . . was the bread, the spiritual bread from heaven that gives life to the world."
>
> —Nancy Guthrie[3]

PRACTICE REMINDER

If you haven't done so already, set aside about thirty minutes sometime this week to prayerfully go through the journaling prompts in the practice section on pages 123–124.

Day 4
Write It Down and Tell the Story

Read Exodus 17:8–16.

As the Israelites continued their journey through the desert, they faced many challenges. We've already seen how they struggled to find food and water and how the Lord faithfully and miraculously provided for them. In this account we witness another challenge that faced them—an attack by a generations-old enemy, the Amalekites. The Amalekites and the Israelites were descendants from the same family, but a betrayal between brothers caused a division that separated and removed them from the rest of the nation of Israel. The deep hurt and anger this conflict created had never been reconciled, as we will see in this passage.

If you want to learn more about this conflict, you can read about these two brothers, Jacob and Esau, and what happened in Genesis 25:19–35 and all of chapter 27.

8. Moses tells Joshua to choose some men and to go fight the Amalekites. What does Moses say he will do while Joshua and the men are fighting (Exodus 17:9)? What is significant about the staff of God (4:17)? Do you think Joshua knew this context? If so, how might this have encouraged him?

9. Under each person's name, record what their role was in the battle and what happened as a result (17:10–13).

Joshua	Moses
Aaron	Hur

10. In the verse below, underline the two things the Lord tells Moses to do now that the battle is over. Then circle the word *remembered*.

Then the LORD said to Moses, "Write this on a scroll as something to be remembered and make sure that Joshua hears it, because I will completely blot out the name of Amalek from under heaven." (Exodus 17:14)

Why do you think it's important for Moses to write down this account? Why do you think it's important for Joshua to hear the story even though he was there and fought in the battle?

11. We don't know, but how do you think Joshua might have remembered the battle without Moses's account?

12. Think through a trial or battle you're witnessing or have re- cently witnessed someone walk through. How might your perspective on God's faithfulness to them be different from their own? Prayerfully ask the Lord how you might share with them something encouraging from your perspective and then make a plan to do what comes to mind.

13. Moses led the Israelites for many years after their exodus from Egypt, and throughout that time he often called them to remember God's faithfulness. Look up the following verses and record what Moses does to help the people remember what the Lord has done or is asking them to do.

Exodus 24:4	
Exodus 24:7a	
Exodus 34:27–28	
Numbers 33:1–2	

Based on these verses and Exodus 17, what two things are important to do to help us remember?

14. Have you ever written down the stories of God's faithfulness in your life? If so, locate an old journal and spend a few minutes reading one of these stories from your past. What differences did you notice between what you currently remember and what you had written? What impact did reading this story have on you?

PRACTICE REMINDER

Think about a recent time when God proved his
faithfulness to you. Spend a few minutes writing
this story down. Note: This is the same exercise
we did in the practice section. If you haven't done
the journaling exercise yet, consider doing it now.
If you have, consider spending five to ten minutes
journaling about a different memory.

My Story of God's Faithfulness

Day 5
The Real Danger in Forgetting

Read Deuteronomy 8:7–18.

This passage in Deuteronomy jumps ahead in Moses's story about forty years. In this account, Moses had led the Israelites through the desert and they were about to move into the promised land. The Lord knew there was real danger for the Israelites if they forgot their journey with him. So while this passage jumps ahead in Moses's story, it's important to study here because it teaches us about the real danger in forgetting God's faithfulness.

15. How is the land described in Deuteronomy 8:7–9? What two things did the Israelites repeatedly complain about in the desert? (See Exodus 15:24 and 16:2–3 for a reminder.) Would these two things be an issue in the new land?

16. What could ultimately happen if the Israelites started to forget (Deuteronomy 8:12–14)? How will this pride manifest itself according to verse 17? How are we prone to do this today?

17. Is it easier to follow God when you are experiencing ease and abundance or hardship and scarcity? Why do you think this is the case?

18. Ask God to show you where you may be trusting in your own efforts to protect and provide for yourself more than God. Write a prayer below confessing this to God and praising him for what he has provided for you.

19. God gave Moses three ways to remember. Write the three ways in the chart below. (If you need help remembering, look back at questions 5 and 10.) Next, brainstorm ways you could practically do these three things in your life. Circle one that you want to do this week. Share with your group how you plan to do it.

God Told Moses to Remember by	I Will Remember by

20. This lesson offered you the opportunity to participate in each of the ways God told Moses to remember: writing the memory, telling the story, and identifying a tangible memento. If you were able to do all three, which one was most impactful to you? Why? How has remembering encouraged you to look for God's faithful guidance in both your present and your future? Are there other strategies that help you remember? If so, what are they?

Recording our significant God-moments reminds us that God is faithful, that he loves us, and that he has a plan even when our life feels like it is in turmoil. When we can readily draw upon God's past faithfulness, we can better rest in his present faithfulness. So the next time you have a significant God-moment, make a point to record it. You never know when you might need that memory to encourage you.

And now, can I encourage you? Look how far you've come—seven lessons down and only three more to go. Great work! We still have some significant things to learn from Moses. And you need to hear the rest of his story. So let's keep at it. Ask the Lord to help you finish strong. I'm praying for you too.

PRACTICE REFLECTION

1. Were you able to complete the journaling activity this week? Why or why not?

2. Was there any aspect of this exercise that surprised you? If so, what was it?

3. What impact, if any, did this exercise have on your relationship with God? Did it impact any other relationships? How?

MENTORING REDEFINED

Day 1

Practice—Mentoring Conversations

What's the first thought or emotion that comes to mind when you hear the word *mentoring*?

Until a few years ago, the words *guilt* and *forced* were the first things that came to my mind.

As a young twentysomething Christian, I had a deep desire to have an older woman invest in my life. So I signed up for the mentoring program at our church. I was paired with a lovely woman who I liked a lot but didn't really click with. Ultimately, the relationship failed. We met for coffee a few times, but it always felt forced, obligatory, and unnatural. Since we didn't complete the program we signed up for, I was left feeling guilty and with questions about what I had done wrong. She probably felt the same way.

After that experience, whenever someone mentioned mentoring I broke into a cold sweat. Images of forced programmatic relationships flooded my mind. Thankfully, my perception of mentoring has changed.

Previously I thought it meant a structured program with one mentor and one mentee who met exclusively over a long period

of time. And while I believe that these longer mentoring relationships are effective for many people, I've come to embrace
the truth that most of us just need some well-placed mentoring
conversations in our lives. This could look like a one-time coffee with the mom whose kids are older than yours or lunch with
a professional woman who is ahead of you in her career. Pretty
much anyone can become a mentor when their experience and
expertise are ahead of our own. We just need to take the initia-
tive and invite them to speak into our lives around the issues we
are wrestling with. But it's not just about us being mentored;
there's also an army of women coming behind us who need our
wise counsel and perspectives. One of the young women I have
mentoring conversations with is a mom in seminary. She will
text or call me every once in a while to ask for advice or just
tell me she's struggling to get it all done. She knows I walked
a similar road a few years before her, so I can offer encouragement, perspective, and prayer. We don't meet regularly or even
talk that often, but I've become a mentor to her in this area of
her life.

This week our practice is to make a simple plan to pursue a
mentoring conversation with a woman ahead of you and a woman
behind you. As you prepare for this practice, I want to encourage
you to be realistic about what fits in your life. Consider what
you are already doing that you could invite someone to join you
in. For example, you could take a coworker to lunch, walk the
dog with your neighbor, or even carpool with a friend to a place
you both go. Perhaps you already know exactly who you want
to talk to, but if you don't, then start with prayer. Ask God to
bring some names to mind. Then make a realistic plan for how
you will have an intentional conversation with these two women
in the near future.

Of the two conversations, it's a lot easier to initiate time with
someone you would like to have mentor you. You can even tell
her your intention is to pick her brain on how she managed a certain situation in her life. However, when you are setting up time
with someone behind you, you may feel you need to tell her why.
If so, just tell her you want to get to know her better. Your aim is

simply to invest in her, not to offer advice that she isn't seeking. Simply take an interest in her and her life.

Your goal is simple: invite women into mentoring conversations. You aren't making a lifelong commitment. Just enjoy a little time with someone while you ask intentional questions, listen well, and offer advice sparingly. And in case she has baggage like I did, maybe don't mention the word *mentoring*.

The person ahead of me that God brought to mind is:

I plan to connect with her by:

The date I will do this by is:

The person behind me that God brought to mind is:

I plan to connect with her by:

The date I will do this by is:

Day 2
Preparation

Read Exodus 18:5–27; 24:12–18; 33:7–11.

> *As you read these passages, write down anything that stands out to you along with any questions you may have.*

Remember the intense season I told you about at the beginning of our study? Graduate school, new job, new community, and then my husband's shattered ankle. I was already near my breaking point, and the added strain of his injury was about to finish the job. I found myself with too many people relying on me, too many tasks to accomplish, and definitely not enough patience or time to manage anything well.

That's when some wise friends stepped in and mentored me. One counseled me to get practical help by grabbing prepared foods and accepting or hiring help wherever I could. Another asked how I was caring for myself and gave me wise tips on letting the nonessentials slide to make sure I was resting. Even my new boss stepped in and coached me through some practical steps on working smarter, not harder. All of these people saw I was at my limit and about to crash, so they stepped in and helped me slow down and cope. It didn't make the journey easy, but it did help me make it through. Eventually the boxes got unpacked, my husband's cast came off, the kids made friends, and I graduated. Life returned to normal . . . or at least a new normal.

Moses got pushed beyond his capacity too. He bore the weight of caring for an often immature and highly needy group of people who had become immobilized by their interpersonal problems. So Moses stepped in and took on the role of judge to help an estimated two million people seek God's will and settle their disagreements. Did you catch that? Two million people. That's a lot of potential disputes.

Was it wise for Moses to take on this much responsibility? No, of course not. No one person can mediate for two million people. Thankfully, Jethro, an older, wiser man, stepped in and spoke this truth over Moses. Jethro served as a needed mentor for Moses.

And then, as we will see, Moses turned around and did the same for Joshua, a young man coming behind him. Moses was mentored and then he became a mentor, and he needed both relationships to fulfill God's calling on his life. We are also called to mentor and to be mentored, to give and take and learn in community as we seek to be the body of Christ in the world. Let's discover some practical tips from Moses's journey for how we can do this well.

PRACTICE REMINDER

If you haven't done so already, make a plan to initiate a mentoring conversation with a woman ahead of you and a woman behind you.

Day 3
Moses's Mentor—Jethro

Read Exodus 18:5–8, 13–27.

At the end of last week, we jumped ahead in the story of Moses so we could study some additional Scripture passages on why God's people needed to remember what he had done for them. In this week's lesson, we will head back to the account that happened just after the Amalekites attacked the Israelites in the desert.

In this passage Jethro, Moses's father-in-law, had heard of all the Lord had done for Moses and the people of Israel (Exodus 18:1) and so he went to see Moses. It's hard to say how long or

※

"Now Jethro, the priest of Midian and father-in-law of Moses, heard of everything God had done for Moses and for his people Israel, and how the LORD had brought Israel out of Egypt." —Exodus 18:1

even if Zipporah, Moses's wife, and their two sons were with Moses on the exodus journey or if they were with Jethro in Midian. The text is inconclusive. However, Moses did at some point send Zipporah and their sons to see her father, and in this passage Jethro is bringing them back to Moses.

1. How does Moses greet Jethro (18:7)? What do you think Moses's actions toward Jethro signify about their relationship? What does Moses do next (verse 8)? How much does Moses tell Jethro?

2. Consider Moses's relationship and past with Jethro (Exodus 2:15–3:1; 4:18). How do you think they each felt about seeing each other?

3. What role does verse 13 say Moses took on the next day? How long did he do this? We don't know for certain, but what kind of disputes do you think Moses was settling?

4. Jethro observes Moses in his new role and then discusses it with Moses. In the conversation bubbles below, write their conversation in your own words (8:14–18).

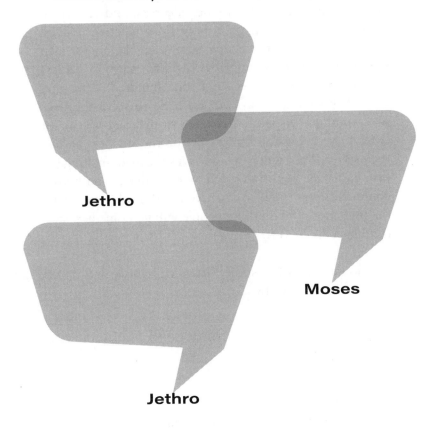

Jethro

Moses

Jethro

5. After Jethro raises his concern and hears Moses's reasoning, he offers some advice. Read the passage on the next page and make the following observations:

• Underline what Jethro encourages Moses to keep doing.

• Put a square around the new thing Jethro advises him to start doing.

• Circle all the potential positive outcomes Jethro gives as reasons for making this change.

Now listen to me, and let me give you a word of advice, and may God be with you. You should continue to be the people's representative before God, bringing their disputes to him. Teach them God's decrees, and give them his instructions. Show them how to conduct their lives. But select from all the people some capable, honest men who fear God and hate bribes. Appoint them as leaders over groups of one thousand, one hundred, fifty, and ten. They should always be available to solve the people's common disputes, but have them bring the major cases to you. Let the leaders decide the smaller matters themselves. They will help you carry the load, making the task easier for you. If you follow this advice, and if God commands you to do so, then you will be able to endure the pressures, and all these people will go home in peace. (Exodus 18:19–23 NLT)

Who does Jethro assume Moses will check with before he takes any advice (18:23)?

Why do you think this is important?

6. Can you think of a time when you did or did not check with God after receiving someone's advice? What was the outcome?

7. What do you think about the advice Jethro gave Moses? Why do you think Moses was unable to think of this idea on his own?

8. Verse 24 says, "Moses listened to his father-in-law and did everything he said." Why do you think Moses was willing to receive Jethro's advice? How do you think Moses felt about the advice?

Thankfully Moses listened to Jethro's advice. If he hadn't, he would have quickly been crushed under the burden he was shouldering. However, even good advice can fall on deaf ears when we aren't ready for it. We might be too caught up in our own way of doing things, don't want to admit there is a better way, or just aren't ready to hear what someone else has to say. Our hearts need to be ready to receive the advice we are given. Moses recognized he needed a new way to do things so he was ready to receive Jethro's words.

9. Think through some times when you've received good advice like Moses did from Jethro. Fill in the blanks based on your experience.

A time when I received advice well was when:

It was well received because:

A time when I did not receive advice well was when:

It was not well received because:

10. According to this passage and your own experience, what are some important things to consider before deciding whether you should or should not take someone's advice?

11. Do you have any Jethroes in your life? Who are they and what are these relationships like? How have they been able to help you discern and follow God's calling in your life? If you don't have any Jethroes, how can you start cultivating some of these relationships?

I have many mentors, or Jethroes, in my life. I have regular conversations with some and others I only talk to once in a while. But each has a unique perspective, background, gift, or skill and can often help me see my issue from a fresh perspective when I get caught in the weeds of my life. —Jodie

---

PRACTICE REMINDER

If you haven't done so already, make a plan to initiate a mentoring conversation with a woman ahead of you and a woman behind you.

Day 4
Moses's Mentee—Joshua

Read Exodus 24:12–18; 33:7–11.

In this section, we are going to move ahead a bit in Moses's story so we can follow the natural progression of being mentored, that is, that we begin mentoring someone else. We first met Moses's mentee and successor, Joshua, in Exodus 17:9, when Moses selected him to lead the battle against the Amalekites. In the months and years following this battle, Moses began the process of intentionally investing in Joshua. This investment becomes critical preparation for Joshua, since he is God's chosen successor to lead Israel when Moses passes away.

This passage happens after Moses had made multiple trips up Mount Sinai to meet with God and to receive his covenant law, encapsulated in the Ten Commandments. This particular trip up the mountain was to receive the stone tablets that were inscribed with the previously given Ten Commandments.

12. It's unclear how far Joshua goes with Moses, but he goes farther than anyone else. How long was Joshua on the mountain (24:18)? Based on the passage, what are some of the things you think Joshua saw and experienced even if just from afar? What do you think Joshua learned from this experience?

13. During the years that the Israelites traveled from Egypt to the promised land, Moses regularly met with and spoke to God in the tent of meeting. After these conversations, Moses would return to the camp and Joshua would stay behind. Again, we don't know what Joshua got to witness in Moses's encounters with the Lord, but he was closer than anyone else. What do you think Joshua might have learned from being this close to Moses and God in the tent of meeting? How do you think this impacted Joshua's relationship with the Lord?

"God would speak to Moses face to face, as a man speaks with his friend (v. 11), that is, clearly and openly. Moses' speaking 'face to face' with God does not contradict the fact that he was not allowed to see God's face (v. 20) as 'face to face' is a figurative expression suggesting openness and friendship."

—John D. Hannah[1]

14. Moses didn't create special opportunities to invest in Joshua; instead, Moses invited Joshua to join him in what he was already doing. Write down some of the activities you do throughout the week (cooking, shopping, exercise, errands, this Bible study, etc.). Consider the woman behind you who you thought of in the practice section. Would any of these activities interest her? How could you invite her into what you are already doing? How can you intentionally model for her what it looks like to follow God's leading in your everyday life?

15. Think through times when you have had the opportunity to invest in someone's life like Moses did for Joshua. Fill in the spaces based on your experience.

A time when my input or investment was well received was:

I think this was because:

A time when my input or investment was not well received was:

I think this was because:

16. Is there something you would do differently the next time you have the opportunity to invest in or give input into some aspect of someone's life? If so, what is it and why?

"An intentional mentor facilitates quality conversations. As you listen with purpose, eventually guide the conversation beyond what happened and who did what. Ask good questions that bring out what is going on inside your mentee. . . . Make no assumptions and give no advice at this point; only listen."
—Sue Edwards and Barbara Neumann[2]

PRACTICE REMINDER

If you haven't done so already, make a plan to initiate a mentoring conversation with a woman ahead of you and a woman behind you.

Day 5
Moses's Final Mentoring Instructions

Read Deuteronomy 6:4–9.

17. Years later, just before Moses's death, he gave some final instructions to the people of Israel, pleading with them to follow God even after Moses was no longer able to lead them. According to 6:7–9, what did Moses instruct the peo-

ple to do with God's commands? How does this verse apply to us today? How could it apply to more than just parents and children?

18. Deuteronomy 6:7 says, "Impress them on your children." Look up the word *impress* in a dictionary and write the definition below. Considering this definition and the sidebar, how can you impress the truths you know about God onto others, based on this verse? What does this kind of relationship look like to you?

> The Hebrew word for "impress" is *shaman* and can be translated as "whet" or "sharpen" or "teach diligently."[3]

"Moses first wrote these words for parents to help them pass on their faith to their children, but they apply equally well to us as mentors mandated to guide our spiritual children on those invisible highways."

—Sue Edwards and Barbara Neumann[4]

19. Do you think Moses lived out Deuteronomy 6:4–9 with Joshua? If so, how?

Deuteronomy 6:4–9 is known as the Shema (Hebrew for "hear") and was recited as a daily confession of faith by pious Jews.[5]

20. Choose one or more of the following biblical mentor-mentee pairs to study. What additional insights can you learn from these passages about mentoring relationships? How did both people in the mentoring relationship encourage the other to choose God's calling in their lives? Share these with your group.

Naomi and Ruth
Ruth 1:6–18; 2:17–3:6; 4:13–17

Eli and Samuel
1 Samuel 3

Elizabeth and Mary
Luke 1:39–56

Paul (previously known as Saul) and Barnabas
Acts 9:26–31; 11:19–26; 13:1–3; 14:1–3

"In a mentoring relationship, most young women are drawn to the . . . model we observe in the *Shema*. Moses favored this biblical approach for transformational impact. Younger women look for older women who will include them in their daily routines, talk about current challenges over coffee, and be available . . . when needs arise. No prep time required."

—Sue Edwards and Barbara Neumann[6]

21. Summarize what you've learned about mentoring from this lesson. Based on this, are there things you feel led to change in some of your current relationships? If so, what are they?

Mentoring relationships are important, but they don't just happen. They take intentionality.

Hopefully through this lesson you were encouraged to be intentional in the spheres and activities where you already find yourself. Chances are you know a lot of women you can invest in or who would be willing to invest in you. A positive mentoring relationship that fosters mutual dependence on God can start with just a few intentional questions. Perhaps start with, "Tell me how you did that," regarding a situation you're facing.

You've only got two more lessons to go. Keep up the good work. Ask God to help you stay the course and finish strong. Or, if you're struggling, ask him to help you recommit to this study of his Word. You can do this! I'm cheering you on.

PRACTICE REFLECTION

1. Who came to mind as someone to reach out to who is ahead of you and why? Who came to mind as someone to reach out to who is behind you and why? Were you surprised that either of these people came to mind? Why or why not?

2. If you were able to reach out to either of these people, how did it go?

3. Did this practice bring you energy and excitement or make you break into a sweat? Why?

BEATEN DOWN BY BETRAYAL

Day 1
Practice—Praying for Your Betrayer

I remember sitting across the table from her. The conversation had started fine, but then it took a turn for the worse. Confusion and shock began to flow through my body. I couldn't understand why she would say those things to me—about me. I knew she was hurt, but I felt absolutely bewildered by the words coming out of her mouth and the fact that they were aimed at me. I felt betrayed and rejected. And then I felt angry.

People can be really hurtful. It's been said that hurt people hurt people. It was true in this instance; she was hurt and now she was hurting me. We've all experienced it and I'm pretty sure we've all done it too, even if unintentionally.

After this episode, she moved on and I was left stewing in the poison of my own hurt and anger. And that made me even angrier.

Things didn't change until I spent some intentional time sitting with the Lord asking him to help me. He helped me process through what was said and helped me replace what I heard with his truths about me. And then he reminded me of his grace and invited me to extend this same grace toward her. This was hard. I'll be honest and tell you, I didn't want to be gracious toward her. She hadn't owned up to what she had done, and I wasn't sure I was ready to let go of the pain she had caused me. But the Lord kept reminding me that the only one I was hurting was me. The bitterness I was letting take root in my soul was eating *me* alive, not her. She had moved on. As far as I know, she hadn't given me or this episode a second thought.

Slowly I began praying for her. I started asking the Lord to bless her. It wasn't easy. And yet, something profound started to happen as I did. My heart started to soften toward her. I started to release her and forgive her. I even started to embrace and appreciate more of God's grace toward my own careless actions and words.

Our relationship was never restored; she didn't want that and it would have been unhealthy for me to make it happen. But by the grace of God and through intentional work on my part, I was able to find healing and peace which eventually led to my own freedom. This episode and her words would not define me—God would.

This week, I invite you into the difficult yet freeing process of praying for someone who has hurt and betrayed you. Chances are you can come up with more than one name, but I want to encourage you to be intentional to just pray for one person this week. The first person who comes to mind is probably the person you need to choose. Their name coming to mind may mean you have a little more work to do in releasing them and finding freedom from the hurt they've caused.

To do this practice, spend intentional time every day praying for this person. Don't just tack it on to the end of your prayer time; really pray for them. Pray for their health, well-being, and relationship with the Lord. Pray that God would bless them and the work of their hands. Pray that your heart would start to soften toward this person and that you would begin to feel freedom and love whenever you think of them or interact with them. There is really no magic formula for how you should do this. Just pray as the Lord leads you.

I'm praying that by the end of this week, your prayers will lead you to experience more freedom when it comes to this person and the hurt they have caused you.

Day 2
Preparation

Read Exodus 32; Numbers 12:1–15.

> *As you read these passages, write down anything that stands out to you along with any questions you may have.*

Moses knew the deep disappointment of hurt and rejection. He was betrayed by two people who should have stood by his side no matter what: his brother, Aaron, and his sister, Miriam. They had been with him every step of the way through the exodus journey. Aaron had served as Moses's spokesperson, which means he was by his side almost everywhere he went (Exodus 4:14–16). And Miriam led the Israelites in worship as soon as they crossed through the Red Sea (Exodus 15:20–21). These two people had not only been with Moses, but they had stood alongside him in solidarity and support for the mission God had given him. And then, for some reason, they turned away. First Aaron turned away from God and then later they both rejected Moses. Why would they do that?

Moses, for the most part, handled it well. It's not that he didn't get frustrated or mad—he did. But he also went to the Lord. He even interceded on their behalf and asked God to show mercy toward them. Moses actually advocated for his betrayers. I think that took a lot of strength and personal security.

We have a lot to learn from Moses and how he navigated these intense relational rejections and disappointments. My prayer is that we will not just observe Moses's reactions, but we will learn from them and allow them to shape how we move forward with

God's purposes in our lives when we find ourselves betrayed by others.

PRACTICE REMINDER

If you haven't done so today, pray for someone who has hurt and betrayed you.

Day 3
Aaron's Betrayal

Read Exodus 32.

Before we dive into this passage, let's do a quick recap so we know where we are in the story. At this point, the people had been rescued from Egypt and were on their way to the promised land. The Lord, in his wisdom, sent them the long way around. During that time the people started to complain quickly due to lack of water and food, which doesn't seem totally unreasonable, and yet the way they went about it was not best. God, in his grace and mercy, continued to provide for all their needs through Moses.

God also gave the people his covenant law during this time as a way to establish how they should operate in their relationship with him and with each other. The law was summarized in the Ten Commandments, which Moses took Joshua up to Mount Sinai to receive.

It's important to note that right before Moses and Joshua made this journey up the mountain, the people had committed to obey everything the Lord had commanded them (Exodus 24:7). This passage in Exodus 32 focuses on what the people were doing while Moses and Joshua were away on the mountain with God.

1. The people ask Aaron to make them a god because they
   don't know what has happened to Moses. Even though Moses was gone, what evidence of God's presence and faithfulness was still evident for the people (16:35; 24:15–17)?

2. How does Aaron respond (32:2–6)? Does he seem hard to
   convince? What surprises you most about his response?

3. According to Exodus 24:18, Moses was on the mountain
   for forty days. Does that seem like a long time to you? Have
   you ever been in a season of uncertainty and waiting before? How long did it last? Does this change your perspective on how the Israelites reacted?

4. Aaron had to choose between pleasing people and pleasing
   God. Think about a time when you had to make this choice
   and, like Aaron, chose people over God. Why do you think
   you did this? What were the consequences to your actions?

After Aaron made the calf, he built an altar and announced a
festival to the Lord (Exodus 32:5). A note from my NIV Study

Bible says, "Apparently Aaron recognized the idolatrous consequences of his deed and acted quickly to keep the people from completely turning away from the Lord."[1] It didn't work though. The festival ended with the people getting up to "indulge in revelry" (32:6), which most likely means they had an orgy. Instead of fixing the problem, they made it worse. They've now broken two commandments: the second—idolatry—and the seventh—adultery (20:4–6, 14).

This whole incident reminds me that I can't cover up my sins from yesterday with a few righteous acts for today. God is the only one who can truly fix my sin problem, and thankfully he does that through Jesus. However, the Israelites lived before Jesus, and so God handles the situation differently.

> Don't forget: If you are a believer in Christ, you've been forgiven for your sins. If you still feel guilt over your actions, ask God to help you accept the forgiveness you've been given and move forward. Still need convincing? Start with these verses: Romans 8:1; Ephesians 1:7–8; Philippians 3:13.

5. God, who was fully aware of what Aaron and the people were doing at the foot of the mountain, told Moses what was happening (Exodus 32:7–10). What does God say he wanted to do to the people? What does he say he would do with Moses? Do you think this offer was at all tempting to Moses?

6. What does Moses ask the Lord to do (verses 11–13)? How does the Lord respond (verse 14)? How does this challenge or encourage you in your prayer life regarding people who may have strayed from the Lord?

∗⁄∗

"Occasionally, my wife has called me at work and asked me to pick up a gallon of milk on my way home. When this happens, I take a different route than I would normally, but I end up at home nonetheless. Perhaps this is similar to how our praying affects God as he carries out his will."

—Dr. Thomas L. Constable[2]

· · · · · · ·

7. Once Moses sees for himself what's been happening, how does he respond (verse 19)? Why do you think his response changes from when God told him earlier about what was going on?

∗⁄∗

"The reference to God 'chang[ing] His mind' (v. 14) has been a problem to many Bible readers. The expression implies no inconsistency or mutability in the character of God. . . . Within the plan of God, however, He has incorporated enough flexibility so that, in most situations, there are a number of options that are acceptable to him."

—Dr. Thomas L. Constable[3]

· · · · · · ·

8. Next Moses turns to Aaron for an explanation. Write their conversation in your own words in the conversation bubbles on the next page (verses 21–24). Compare Aaron's answer with what really happened (verses 1–4). In the second set of bubbles, write what you think Aaron would have said if he were being truthful.

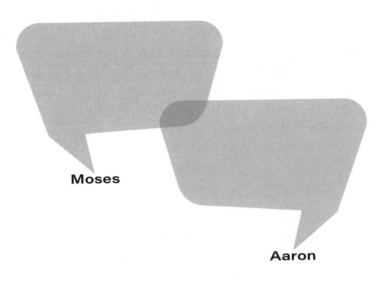

"In anger Moses . . . smashed the tablets of the Law, symbolizing the people's breaking of the covenant. Second, he burned the idol, reduced it to powder, spread it on water . . . and made the people drink it. By this action he demonstrated both the powerlessness of the calf-idol and God's wrath. . . . Drinking it symbolized that the people had to bear the consequences of their sin."

—John D. Hannah[4]

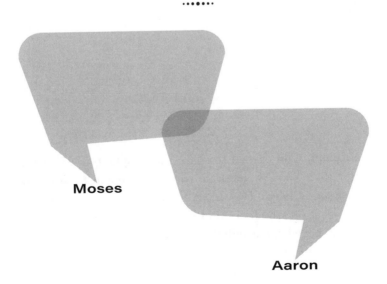

9. Have you ever been like Aaron and gotten caught doing something wrong by someone you are close to? How did you first respond when you were caught? Did the situation impact your relationship? If so, how? How did you eventually reconcile the situation? How do you wish you had responded differently?

10. Have you ever been like Moses and caught someone else doing wrong? What did you do when you caught them? If you confronted the person, how did they respond? Do you wish they had responded differently? If so, how? How did this impact your relationship?

11. How might Moses have felt betrayed by Aaron due to this incident? What are some other ways it could have impacted their relationship?

Even though God agreed to spare the people, there is still a cost for their sin. About three thousand people were put to death (Exodus 32:28). How heartbreaking this must have been for Aaron. If only he had said no to the initial request, maybe this could have been avoided. —Jodie

12. Read Exodus 32:31–32 and Deuteronomy 9:18–20. Both of these are accounts of Moses's second intercessory prayer regarding this incident. How did Moses intercede for the people? What did he say to God about what he wanted if God wouldn't forgive them? What do you think this says about how he cared for the people?

Moses told God that if He refused to forgive His people he would prefer to have his name removed from the book God had written (Ex. 32:32). Some say this was the book of life (Rev. 20:15; 21:27) that lists believers' names but, more likely, it was the census of the people. Moses' statement probably indicated he was willing to die a premature death (but not suffer eternal torment in hell).

—John D. Hannah[5]

13. Based on what you've learned about how Moses responded to this incident, is there something you feel you should do in regard to those who have either betrayed you or strayed from the Lord? If so, what? If you feel comfortable, share this with your group for prayer and accountability.

PRACTICE REMINDER

If you haven't done so today, pray for someone who has hurt and betrayed you.

Day 4
Miriam and Aaron's Betrayal

Read Numbers 12:1–15.

You would hope that after the issue with the golden calf, Aaron had learned a few things about trusting the Lord and remaining in solidarity with Moses's leadership. Unfortunately, as we will see, that didn't fully happen. Not long after they left Sinai, tensions started to rise again. The people continued to grumble and complain, and this time Miriam and Aaron joined in.

This account is in Numbers, which is the fourth book in your Bible. It is written by Moses and continues to tell portions of the story of Israel's journey from slavery to freedom. One of the main themes of Numbers is Israel's continued rebellion and unbelief toward God, which eventually resulted in the consequence of the Israelites having to spend forty years wandering in the desert.

14. What do Miriam and Aaron do in 12:1–2? What do you think was fueling their words?

15. Think back to a time when you have been critical of someone else. Why were you critical of this person? What happened to make you feel this way?

16. What did God do about this situation (Numbers 12:4–12)? Why do you think only Miriam was struck with leprosy (verse 10)? Why do you think their actions were such a big deal to God? What was Moses's response (verse 13)?

We don't really know why Miriam was struck with leprosy and not Aaron. Theologians have tried to speculate, but in the end it's still speculation. Here's what you do need to know. Miriam was not treated differently because she was a woman. She was treated differently because she must have had a different role in the betrayal than Aaron did. God values men and women the same and he treats all our sin equally as sin. We won't know the specific reasons for Miriam's leprosy until we get to heaven. But in the meantime, we can trust what we do know about the character of our God—he is loving and gracious. And somehow in this act he was being true to his character.

17. How do you think Moses felt when he heard that Miriam and Aaron had been "talking against" him?

18. Have you ever been in a similar situation where you found out someone betrayed you by speaking critically of you? What happened? How did you feel when you found out?

If you haven't done so today, pray for someone
who has hurt and betrayed you.

Day 5
Responding to Betrayal

Read Matthew 5:43–48.

Moses exemplified how to respond to the betrayal of others through his intercession on their behalf. Jesus underscored
Moses's actions with these words, "Love your enemies and pray
for those who persecute you" (Matthew 5:44). Yet we all know
from our own experience that this couldn't have been an easy
task for Moses. It's much easier to love our friends and pray for
those who are kind to us. But often the good work God calls us
to do is the difficult work of loving and praying for those who it's
hardest to love and pray for. And in God's grace and goodness,
it's often through doing this hard work that we find true healing.
Let's take one more look at how and why we should pray for others and some of the results that come when we do.

19. According to Matthew 5:43–48, what are some reasons we
    should love and pray for our enemies? Knowing that Jesus
    isn't talking about our eternal salvation in this passage,
    what are some potential rewards (5:46) we could receive
    when we love and pray for our enemies?

20. Moses went to God multiple times on behalf of those who had betrayed either God or him. Fill in the chart below regarding these situations and how Moses interceded on their behalf.

Verse(s)	Who Moses Interceded For	Specific Request Made
Exodus 32:12	the nation	relent: don't bring disaster on them
Exodus 32:31–32		
Deuteronomy 9:20		
Numbers 12:10–13		

21. God answered each of the prayers that Moses prayed. Why do you think God answered his prayers (see John 15:7; 1 John 5:14–15)? How does this encourage or challenge you?

22. Praying for someone who has betrayed us is no easy task, yet Moses was able to do it. Why do you think that was?

Think of a few people in your life who have hurt or betrayed you. How could you specifically pray for them? Write some ideas in the chart below (feel free to use your own code if writing their names feels too vulnerable to you). The next time this person crosses your mind, commit to praying one of these things for them.

Name	How I Can Pray

23. Who do the following verses say intercedes for you: Romans 8:27, 34, and Hebrews 7:24–25? As you challenge yourself to pray for those who have hurt you in some way, how does it make you feel to know that you are also being prayed for? How does knowing this help you process the betrayal in your life and look to God and his good purposes in this season?

Moses cried out to God on behalf of his community and then later for his sister. Jesus also modeled prayer for his enemies when he hung on the cross and in physical anguish looked down upon his tormentors and prayed, "Father, forgive them, for they do not know what they are doing" (Luke 23:34). These tender words spoken over those who did not deserve them give me strength and courage to pray similar words. May I offer you a prayer for yourself and those who have hurt you, if you need a place to start?

> *Lord, they have no idea how much they have hurt me. And yet you do. You see me, know me, and love me. Lord, would you speak truth into my heart and mind about this situation? Remind me of who I am in you. Heal the broken places in my heart. And Lord, heal the broken places in their heart. They know not what they do. Draw near to them and shower them with your healing and redemptive love. Lord, would you bring them abundant blessings in your name today? And may my heart rejoice when good happens in their life. I release them to your love and care today. Amen.*

We have one lesson left. Can you believe it? Keep up the great work and finish strong.

PRACTICE REFLECTION

1. Were you able to identify and pray for someone who has betrayed you? Why or why not?

2. Did you notice any changes in your heart as you prayed for your betrayer this week? If so, describe what happened. If not, why do you think that is?

LEAVING A LASTING LEGACY

Day 1
Practice—Celebration

It's time to celebrate!

You're starting the last week of our study and I think that deserves a celebration.

You may not think completing a Bible study is worthy of a celebration, but I do. You've spent time with the Lord. You've prayed intentionally for others. You've asked the Lord what he wants for you. Hopefully you've even taken a few bold steps of obedience along the way. These are not small things. These are actions that lead us closer to Jesus and help us become more like him, and that is worthy of celebration.

One of my close friends has been teaching me how to celebrate over the last few years. She's dragged me to dinner to celebrate a promotion; she's given me cards to celebrate a successful event; she's even texted me a "way to go" message after a hard workout. At first, I resisted her attempts to celebrate. I brushed things off as not being a big deal or because I didn't want the attention. She called me out on my resistance, which led me to reflect on why I was reacting this way. I discovered it was fear. I was afraid that if I celebrated what was good, something negative might creep in to overshadow it. I subconsciously believed the celebratory things in life were limited, temporary, and fragile. I had allowed pessimism and scarcity to become an undercurrent in my life without even knowing it. But through my friend's intentional celebrations, I started to see the goodness of God in a new way. Even when life was hard, there were still good things to take note of and celebrate.

Scripture affirms celebrating. David danced in celebration before the Lord. Elizabeth celebrated Mary's pregnancy. The wise men celebrated Jesus's birth. Even Paul and Silas when imprisoned celebrated with singing to the Lord.

Celebrating helps us move our hearts toward God as we recognize what has been accomplished. It helps us focus, for a moment, on all the good he's given us. And this changes our hearts. Before long we find that no matter our circumstances, we are drawn toward God in praise, worship, and thanksgiving—even in the midst of hard times.

So this week I want to invite you into the intentional practice of celebrating.

To do this practice, start with prayer. Ask the Lord who you could celebrate and why. When he brings someone to mind, ask him for his creativity in how you should celebrate. Go with what you think he is leading you to. It can be big or small, just make sure it is something you can actually pull off in the next week or so and that it feels like a celebration of some kind—even a cupcake or a card can be a celebration. Also, if the Lord brings you to mind as needing to be celebrated, don't be shy about throwing a little party for yourself. The only rule is you can't celebrate alone or secretly.

May you see the goodness of our God as you practice celebrating this week.

Day 2
Preparation

Read Numbers 20:1–13; Deuteronomy 34.

> *As you read these passages, write down anything that stands out to you along with any questions you may have.*

I don't like sad movies. I figure there's enough sad in real life that I don't need to bring make-believe sad into it too. So when I get to choose, I choose feel-good movies. The ones where everything works out, all the conflict is resolved, true love is found, and they skip off into the sunset.

My desire for happy endings may be one of the reasons I've been struggling so much with this last lesson. Moses had a little slipup with God. Actually, in God's eyes it wasn't so little. And it resulted in some big consequences. Moses no longer got to enter the promised land. He got to take the people right up to the edge. He even got to climb a mountain so he could see the whole land. But he did not get to go in—not even one tiny little step.

I know God is God and he doesn't make mistakes, but it still seems unfair. Moses sacrificed, followed, listened, and obeyed. He led a group of whiny, often immature and sometimes even angry people through the desert for forty years. Forty years! That's half a lifetime of wandering around when a straight shot would have only taken a few years. He did a lot of things right—and then he did this one thing wrong. Don't all the right things outweigh this one wrong thing?

And then it hit me. I'm looking at the situation all wrong. I'm focused on the one thing Moses doesn't get and I'm missing the countless things he *did* get. Moses got to talk with God face-to-face, as one talks with a friend (Exodus 33:11). Moses got to perform signs and wonders on God's behalf. Moses got to rescue an entire nation from annihilation. Moses got to preserve the line of the Messiah. Moses got to live such an extraordinary life that Scripture says no one else has had such an experience with God (Deuteronomy 34:10–12). This extraordinary life is Moses's legacy, not his sin.

In the end, I don't think Moses would have traded his journey for anything. I sure wouldn't. I think the journey mattered more to Moses than the final result of entering the promised land.

We still need to take a close look at why Moses was denied entrance into the land, but we can't get stuck there because Moses and the rest of the authors of Scripture didn't get stuck there either.

I'm thankful for this because, like Moses, I've made some pretty big mistakes I'd like to forget about. And yes, there are still consequences for my actions (like no promised land for Moses), but these sins don't define me . . . or you. And these sins don't become our legacy either. Instead, when we sin, God invites us to turn back to him and continue in the calling he has given us. So as you move through this last lesson, may you allow the grace of God to cover over your past mistakes. They do not define you or your legacy.

You have been chosen by God for an extraordinary journey. Choose to follow him as Moses did.

PRACTICE REMINDER

If you haven't done so already, make a plan to intentionally celebrate someone this week.

Day 3
Moses's Sin

Read Numbers 20:1–13.

The Israelite people have been in the wilderness for close to forty years now. That means they've been experiencing God's miraculous, unmistakable, and unfailing provision for forty years. That's a long time. And yet, it seems not much has changed with this grumbling crowd.

1. What problem sent the people to Moses (Numbers 20:2–5)? What did they say to him? How would you describe their attitude?

2. What did Moses do (verse 6)? What exactly did the Lord tell Moses to do (verses 7–8)? How do these instructions compare to the Lord's instructions the last time he brought water from a rock through Moses in Exodus 17:6?

3. According to Numbers 20:9–11, what did Moses do differently than what the Lord instructed? Rewrite in your own words what Moses said to the people before he struck the rock. What do you think Moses's tone of voice and attitude could have been like when he said this? (See Psalm 106:32–33 for additional insight into this moment.)

4. Why do you think Moses got frustrated with the people?

5. What are some situations or people that tend to frustrate you? How do you tend to react in these situations? In what way is your reaction similar or different from Moses's?

6. Why do you think the Lord still brought water out of the rock even though Moses disobeyed what God told him to do?

7. What was the root of Moses and Aaron's sin (Numbers 20:12)? The consequence for this sin was not going into the promised land. Do you think this consequence was appropriate, too easy, or too harsh? Why?

Read Luke 12:48 and James 3:1. How do these verses help you understand why the consequences seemed so steep for Moses?

8. Recall the situations or people that tend to frustrate you and your reactions to them from question 5. What do you think is the root of your reactions? How is this the same or different from Moses and Aaron? What does Proverbs 3:5–6 say will happen when we trust God more fully? How does this verse encourage you in these situations?

⁓

"Moses was supposed to speak to the rock; God had not told him to speak to the people. But Moses rebuked them, setting himself up as their judge, and himself and Aaron as their deliverers, by suggesting that they were the ones who would bring water out of the rock."

—Nancy Guthrie[1]

....

9. Even though Moses sinned, his sin did not define him or his legacy. The same is true for us as followers of Jesus. What do the following verses say is true about you and your legacy?

Romans 8:15–16

2 Corinthians 5:17

1 Peter 2:9

How does this encourage you regarding the situations you listed in questions 5 and 8?

※

"Because the rock represented God himself—the source of water and refreshment to his people—when Moses struck the rock two times in anger, it was 'nothing less than a direct assault on God.'"

—Nancy Guthrie[2]

•••••••

PRACTICE REMINDER

If you haven't done so already, make a plan to intentionally celebrate someone this week.

Day 4
Moses's Final Moments

Read Deuteronomy 34.

We don't know exactly when Moses struck the rock in disobedience, but most scholars believe it happened near the end of the forty years of desert wandering, perhaps even in the last year. Regardless of when it happened, after God told Moses the consequence for his disobedience, he didn't seem to complain or argue. Instead, he moved forward faithfully in what appeared to be acceptance of the consequence. This leads us to the final part of Moses's journey which is recorded in Deuteronomy 34. Moses was 120 years old and in the last moments of his life.

10. What does God show Moses at the top of Mount Nebo (verses 1–3)? What do you think the land looked like (Numbers 13:23, 27)? What does God say to Moses (Deuteronomy 34:4)?

﹡

Deuteronomy, the fifth
and the last book of the
Pentateuch (the five books
of the Law), was written to
encourage and exhort the
Israelites before they enter
into their new life in the
promised land. To that end, it
reminds them of their wilderness wanderings and the law
given at Mount Sinai. It also
ends with the story of Moses's
death.

11. Why do you think God showed
Moses the land? How do you think
it felt for Moses to see this?

For the Israelites, the promised land
was a physical place where they
could begin to enjoy their freedom
and flourish in their relationship
with God and one another. It was
also a fertile land that would abun-
dantly meet all their needs.

12. Imagine what it would look like for you to enter into a
"promised land" that would provide similar flourishing for
you as it did for the Israelites. Describe what this would be
like. While it may not be a physical place, write down any
words, thoughts, and emotions that help you describe it.

13. Do you think you will ever be able to enter into such a
place? Why or why not?

14. Someday Jesus will return and usher in the creation of a

new heaven and a new earth (2 Peter 3:10–13). This will be the ultimate promised land for all believers. Choose a few of the following verses that describe what this new heaven and new earth will be like: John 14:2; Colossians 3:1; Revelation 21:4, 22–27; 22:1–5. Based on these verses, what are you most looking forward to?

15. Think back over the journey Moses had with God. How would you characterize the relationship between Moses and God? How did that relationship change over the course of Moses's life? Do you think the journey and their relationship made it easier for Moses to say goodbye to this world?

16. How has your relationship with the Lord changed over your lifetime? How has this relationship sustained you through mistakes, hardships, and desert seasons in your own life? What steps do you need to take to help your relationship with the Lord continue to grow and develop so it looks more and more like Moses's relationship with the Lord?

"Finally there would be nothing standing between him and the lover of his soul. And this is what I have come to see most clearly in the life of Moses: *for Moses the presence of God was the Promised Land.* Next to that, everything else had already paled in significance."

—Ruth Haley Barton[3]

•••••••

Thankfully, Moses isn't defined by or remembered for his mistakes. Let's discover how Moses was remembered—and choose how we want to be remembered too.

17. Deuteronomy ends with the following epitaph for Moses:

There has never been another prophet in Israel like Moses, whom the LORD knew face to face. The LORD sent him to perform all the miraculous signs and wonders in the land of Egypt against Pharaoh, and all his servants, and his entire land. With mighty power, Moses performed terrifying acts in the sight of all Israel. (Deuteronomy 34:10–12 NLT)

What do these verses say was unique about Moses and why?

How do you hope to be remembered? Spend a few minutes prayerfully thinking about some of the characteristics, roles, and activities you want to be remembered for. Jot them down in the space on the next page. Then, write your epitaph. Start with the pattern set in Deuteronomy by filling in the blanks below. Then finish by writing what else you would want it to say. (For example, I might say: There

has never been another woman in Texas like Jodie. She had
an intimate relationship with the Lord . . .)

There has never been another_____ in_____
like_____. She_____
_____
_____
_____
_____
_____
_____
_____.

Are there changes you need to make to become the woman
you just wrote about? Do you believe God is inviting you
to make any of these changes? If so, what are they? What
is one practical thing you can do this week to move toward
becoming this woman?

18. Deuteronomy 34:10 says, "Since then, no prophet has risen
in Israel like Moses." However, Hebrews tells us that a
greater prophet has now come. According to Hebrews 3:3–
6, who is this greater prophet? What makes him greater
than Moses?

PRACTICE REMINDER

If you haven't done so already, make a plan to
intentionally celebrate someone this week.

Day 5
Moses Remembered: A Man of Faith

Read Hebrews 11:23–29.

Hebrews 11 is sometimes called the "Hall of Faith" or the "Heroes
of the Faith" because it highlights some of the many men and
women throughout Scripture who are commended for their exem-
plary faith.

19. According to Hebrews 11:1, how is *faith* defined?

20. What stands out to you most about Moses's faith as re-
    corded in this passage? Why?

21. Thinking through what we've studied, is there some additional aspect of Moses's faith that impacted you that you would add to the list recorded in Hebrews? If so, what would you add? Why do you think this didn't make the list in Hebrews?

    By faith Moses _____.

22. Think back over your life. What are some things you have done by faith? Fill in some of the blanks below (or add more as you desire) using your name and what you did by faith.

    By faith _____.

    By faith _____.

    By faith _____.

    How does this encourage you?

23. What do you notice is missing from Moses's "by faith" list (Exodus 2:12; 4:13–14; Numbers 20:10–11)?

As far as east is from west—
that's how far God has
removed our sin from us.
(Psalm 103:12 CEB)

Why do you think this is? How does
this encourage you?

Review

24. Now that you have studied Moses's life, what will you re-
    member him for?

25. Is there something you feel the Lord is calling you to do as a
    result of this study? If so, what is it? Share with your group
    for accountability.

Well done! Now it's time for me to celebrate you. If I could bake
you a cupcake, I would. It would be your favorite flavor with
confetti on top and a fun sparkler candle. We'd light it and as
your face glowed in the sparkling light, I would pray this prayer
over you:

Lord, bless my sister. May she know how dearly loved
she is. Would you whisper into her heart how you have
created her, gifted her, and called her to her own extraor-
dinary journey? Would you give her courage to choose to

follow you? Courage to choose to make the hard choices of obedience. Courage to choose to keep her eyes and heart focused on you. Courage to be the woman you are inviting her to be. And would you help her see that her life of faithful obedience matters deeply? May she choose to live her one life well, just as Moses did. Amen.

I believe that when we get to heaven, the hall of faith in Hebrews 11 will have some additions to it. What might it say you did by faith? I can't wait to see. I expect we will be doing some celebrating when we get there.

PRACTICE REFLECTION

1. Who or what did you celebrate and why?

2. Did you find this activity easy, hard, fun, challenging, scary, or something else? Why?

3. How did this activity impact your heart and mind? How did it impact your relationship with God?

ACKNOWLEDGMENTS

All great work is done in teams. This Bible study is no exception. My first thanks always goes to Jesus. Without you, where would we be? Another big thank-you goes to Moses. Thank you for being a real man of faith with real challenges. Thank you for showing us what it means to be faithful and choose to follow God's leading, even when the cost is high.

Thank you to Tim, who supports, cheers, loves, and listens— what a gift. Thank you to my girls for being proud of their mama. Thank you to Tiffany Stein, Jennifer Lewis, and Candice Unger, who were the very first readers of this study and offered thoughtful encouragement and critique. Thank you to the best and most supportive friends a girl could ask for: Cheri Hudspith, Sissy Mathew, and Julie Pierce. Finally, thank you to my church, Irving Bible Church, and especially the women there for studying Moses with me.

NOTES

Week 1: God Is in Control

1. "Sleep Time Recommendations: What's Changed?" sleepfounda tion.com, accessed June 4, 2020, www.sleepfoundation.org/arti cles/how-much-sleep-do-we-really-need.

2. Adele Ahlberg Calhoun, *Spiritual Disciplines Handbook: Practices That Transform Us* (Downers Grove, IL: InterVarsity, 2008), 64.

3. I. Howard Johnson, A. R. Millard, J. I. Packer, and D. J. Wiseman, eds., "pharaoh," *New Bible Dictionary*, 3rd edition (Downers Grove, IL: InterVarsity, 1996), 913.

4. *Merriam-Webster's Collegiate Dictionary*, 10th ed., s.v., "fear," (Springfield, MA: Merriam-Webster, 1996).

5. Iain D. Campbell, *Opening Up Exodus*, Opening Up the Bible (Carlisle, PA: Day One, 2006), 24.

6. John D. Hannah, "Exodus," in J. F. Walvoord and R. B. Zuck, eds., *The Bible Knowledge Commentary: An Exposition of the Scriptures*, vol. 1 (Wheaton, IL: Victor, 1985), 111.

Week 2: Burning Bush Moments

1. Thomas L. Constable, *Notes on Exodus*, 2020 edition, Plano Bible Chapel, planobiblechapel.org/tcon/notes/pdf/exodus.pdf, 33.

2. Constable, *Notes on Exodus*, 40.

3. Priscilla Shirer, *Discerning the Voice of God Bible Study Book* (Nashville: LifeWay, 2006), 33.

4. Henry Blackaby, *Experiencing God* (Nashville: Broadman & Holman, 1998), 56.

5. Shirer, *Discerning the Voice of God Bible Study*, 35–36.

Week 3: The Comfort of Confirmation

1. John D. Hannah, "Exodus," in J. F. Walvoord and R. B. Zuck, eds., *The Bible Knowledge Commentary: An Exposition of the Scriptures*, vol. 1 (Wheaton, IL: Victor, 1985), 113.

Week 4: Dealing with Discouragement

1. *NIV Study Bible* (Grand Rapids: Zondervan, 2011), 103.
2. John D. Hannah, "Exodus," in J. F. Walvoord and R. B. Zuck, eds., *The Bible Knowledge Commentary: An Exposition of the Scriptures*, vol. 1 (Wheaton, IL: Victor, 1985), 156.
3. Iain D. Campbell, *Opening Up Exodus*, Opening Up the Bible (Carlisle, PA: Day One, 2006), 36.

Week 5: From Crisis of Faith to Faithful Obedience

1. James Bryan Smith, *The Good and Beautiful God* (Downers Grove, IL: InterVarsity, 2009), 53.
2. T. P. Pearce, s.v., "Sovereignty of God," in Chad Brand et al., eds., *Holman Illustrated Bible Dictionary* (Nashville: Holman Bible Publishers, 2003), 1523.
3. Victor P. Hamilton, *Handbook on the Pentateuch* (Grand Rapids: Baker Academic, 2005), 164.
4. Hamilton, *Handbook on the Pentateuch*, 165.
5. John D. Hannah, "Exodus," in J. F. Walvoord and R. B. Zuck, eds., *The Bible Knowledge Commentary: An Exposition of the Scriptures*, vol. 1 (Wheaton, IL: Victor, 1985), 119.

Week 6: Preventing Pride

1. Nancy Guthrie, *The Lamb of God: Seeing Jesus in Exodus, Leviticus, Numbers, and Deuteronomy* (Wheaton, IL: Crossway, 2012), 98.
2. Jerry Bridges, *Transforming Grace: Living Confidently in God's Transforming Love* (Colorado Springs: NavPress, 1993), 21–22.
3. Philip Yancey, *What's So Amazing About Grace?* (Grand Rapids: Zondervan, 1997), 71.

Week 7: Remembering Well

1. J. F. Walvoord and R. B. Zuck, eds., *The Bible Knowledge Com-*

mentary: An Exposition of the Scriptures, vol. 1 (Wheaton, IL: Victor, 1985), 13.

2. Nancy Guthrie, *The Lamb of God: Seeing Jesus in Exodus, Leviticus, Numbers, and Deuteronomy* (Wheaton, IL: Crossway, 2012), 102.
3. Guthrie, *The Lamb of God*, 104.

Week 8: Mentoring Redefined

1. John D. Hannah, "Exodus," in J. F. Walvoord and R. B. Zuck, eds., *The Bible Knowledge Commentary: An Exposition of the Scriptures*, vol. 1 (Wheaton, IL: Victor, 1985), 157.
2. Sue Edwards and Barbara Neumann, *Organic Mentoring: A Mentor's Guide to Relationships with Next Generation Women* (Grand Rapids: Kregel, 2014), 129.
3. James Strong, "shaman," *Enhanced Strong's Lexicon* (Ontario, Canada: Woodside Bible Fellowship, 1995).
4. Edwards and Neumann, *Organic Mentoring*, 16.
5. *NIV Study Bible* (Grand Rapids: Zondervan, 2011), 270.
6. Edwards and Neumann, *Organic Mentoring*, 116.

Week 9: Beaten Down by Betrayal

1. *NIV Study Bible* (Grand Rapids: Zondervan, 2011), 144.
2. Thomas L. Constable, *Notes on Exodus*, 2020 edition, Plano Bible Chapel, planobiblechapel.org/tcon/notes/pdf/exodus.pdf, 274.
3. Constable, *Notes on Exodus*, 273.
4. John D. Hannah, "Exodus," in J. F. Walvoord and R. B. Zuck, eds., *The Bible Knowledge Commentary: An Exposition of the Scriptures*, vol. 1 (Wheaton, IL: Victor, 1985), 156.
5. Hannah, "Exodus," 156–57.

Week 10: Leaving a Lasting Legacy

1. Nancy Guthrie, *The Lamb of God: Seeing Jesus in Exodus, Leviticus, Numbers, and Deuteronomy* (Wheaton, IL: Crossway, 2012), 23.
2. Guthrie, *The Lamb of God*, 23.
3. Ruth Haley Barton, *Strengthening the Soul of Your Leadership* (Downers Grove, IL: InterVarsity, 2018), 214. Emphasis in original.

ABOUT THE AUTHOR

Jodie Niznik is the adult ministries pastor at Irving Bible Church in Irving, Texas. She has served in various roles on the pastoral team at her church over the last eleven years, including pastor to women. Her calling and passion is to equip people to take the next step in their journey with Jesus. She loves to write about and teach scriptural truths in practical and easy-to-understand ways.

Jodie has an undergraduate degree in broadcast journalism from the University of Colorado and a master's degree in Christian education with an emphasis in women's ministry from Dallas Theological Seminary. She is also the coauthor of *Galatians: Discovering Freedom in Christ Through Daily Practice* with Sue Edwards.

Jodie is married to Tim. They have two young adult daughters, Taylor and Billie, who attend universities in Oklahoma and Arkansas. Jodie and Tim miss their daughters but love their quiet Saturdays. Jodie believes gummy bears and coffee are sweet gifts from the Lord that provide fuel as she writes Bible studies and prepares biblical teachings.